OUT OF THE
FREEZER
INTO THE
MICROWAVE

OUT OF THE
FREEZER
INTO THE
MICROWAVE

by

ANNETTE YATES

PAPERFRONTS

**ELLIOT RIGHT WAY BOOKS,
KINGSWOOD, SURREY, U.K.**

Made and Printed in Great Britain by
Cox and Wyman Ltd, Reading

CONTENTS

CHAPTER   PAGE

   Introduction   7
1 The microwave-freezer friendship   9
2 Advantages and limitations of the microwave oven   10
3 The microwave oven   13
4 Adapting your own recipes for microwave cooking   15
5 Choosing a microwave oven   18
6 Looking after your microwave oven   21
7 The freezer   23
8 Equipment to use   25
9 A guide to defrosting   32
10 A guide to reheating   43
11 About the recipes   46
12 Conversion tables   48
13 Recipes: Soups and starters   50
        Fish   58
        Vegetables   64
        Sauces   77
        Meat   82
        Poultry   97
        Rice and pasta   104
        Fruit and desserts   109
        Freezer/Microwave snacks   114
        Cooking for one and two   118
   Index   123

ILLUSTRATIONS

FIGURE	PAGE
1 How microwaves heat food	13
2 Reheating. Using a microwave thermometer	17
Shapes and sizes of cooking container	28 to 30

INTRODUCTION

My decision to write this book was made one hectic day two years ago. It was a week when my home and work schedules were particularly busy. On Friday afternoon I had not yet planned the children's tea. Out of the freezer came two small portions of beef casserole which were defrosted and then reheated in the microwave and served with microwave-cooked green beans and jacket potatoes. While my daughters ate I defrosted summer fruits in syrup and shortbread. Without realising it, I was taking for granted the marvellous friendship between my freezer in the garage and the microwave oven on the kitchen worktop.

Later that evening the doorbell rang to produce friends, with bottle of wine in hand, ready for their supper. I had forgotten. My instinct might have been panic but again the appliances came to the rescue. Relaxing during the meal, just under an hour later, I wondered how I used to cope without microwave and freezer – and realised that the first seed of "Out of the Freezer, into the Microwave" had been sown. My Paperfront editor who produced my "Microwave Cooking Properly Explained, with recipes" (currently in its n'th edition) had hit on the identical idea in the same week. That settled it. I was to begin the first draft at once, hand in hand with the creation and testing of recipes that were already deliciously tempting in my mind's-eye.

It is with my sort of busy lifestyle in mind that I have prepared the contents of these pages. In them you will find much information and many useful ideas on using the microwave and freezer – together – to their best advantage. So even when time is at a premium or you are away from home, your diet (and that of your family) need not suffer. Meals can be varied and well-balanced with little effort. Whether you love to cook or spend the least amount of time in the kitchen you will soon find in the microwave oven and the freezer, two indispensable assistants.

There are numerous excellent freezing books on the market. For this reason I have limited details of basic freezing principles and methods in order to concentrate on the use of the two appliances to complement each other. Hopefully you will enjoy trying out the recipes – there are over 50 in the second half of the book. I certainly did.

Finally I would like to thank the Microwave Oven Division of

Toshiba (UK) Ltd., Frimley, Camberley, Surrey for providing their latest microwave oven. Thanks also to Lakeland Plastics Alexandra Buildings, Cumbria, for their help with containers and blanching times, and to Mr. J. G. Davies, M.B.E., Physicist at the Cardiac Department of St. George's Hospital, London SW1 for his advice on the safety of microwave ovens and their possible effect on cardiac pacemakers (page 12). Thanks too to my friend Angela for her patience while typing much of the manuscript, and to my family and friends for their inevitable "recipe testing" over the past two years.

A.Y.

1

THE MICROWAVE/ FREEZER FRIENDSHIP

A microwave oven is a perfect companion to your freezer and vice versa. Your freezer no longer remains just another storage area but becomes part of your system of cooking. At first some extra thought will need to be given to the use of the two appliances in conjunction. No doubt already you will have mastered the art of freezer use (since the majority of people seem to buy a microwave oven to complement their freezer). Once you have grasped the techniques of microwave cooking, the microwave-freezer friendship will only require nurturing. In a short time you will have perfected it to suit your own needs. Do not be put off by mistakes. I still make them. Learn from them and successes will soon outweigh failures.

Our grandmothers had baking days, making a week's supply of bread and cakes. Fruit and vegetables were bottled for the winter months. Laborious hours were spent in the kitchen. Today freezer owners are able to take advantage of their own garden produce, cheap seasonal foods (from the butcher, fishmonger or green-grocer) and bulk purchases. Additionally we all agree that saving time can mean saving money. Food stored in the freezer is ready for immediate use with the speedy defrosting, cooking and/or reheating in the microwave oven. The freezer (particularly if it is well stocked) and the microwave are economical to run too. The speedy cooking of the microwave can mean marked savings on your fuel bills.

Just as freezing is one of the easiest and safest methods of preservation, so is microwaving one of the easiest and safest methods of cooking. Both appliances help produce meals containing foods which have retained the maximum natural colour, quality and flavour. Used in conjunction with your other kitchen equipment, e.g. hob, conventional oven, grill and so on, the combinations with which to produce mouth-watering meals, with a minimum of time "slaving" in the kitchen, are endless.

2

ADVANTAGES AND LIMITATIONS OF THE MICROWAVE OVEN

ADVANTAGES

Speed

This is probably the most obvious advantage. Food may be defrosted, then cooked and/or reheated in one third to one quarter of the time normally taken for each. Some foods are ready in an even shorter time. Here are a few comparisons:

	Microwave cooking time	Conventional cooking time
Chicken leg	4 mins	20 mins
Whole chicken	30 mins	1½ hours
Lamb joint	30 mins	1½ hours
Jacket potato	4 mins	1 hour

Economy

Microwave energy is directed straight into the food. None is wasted heating up the container or even the oven walls. Energy is used only while cooking is taking place – there is no pre-heating as with conventional methods. So the microwave oven uses only about one quarter of the energy normally used by a conventional oven. Cooking for one is particularly economical.

Versatility

A microwave oven does not only reheat foods. That is a popular misconception. In this one appliance you can cook from fresh ready to eat or freeze; you can defrost frozen food and then cook it; you can also speed up many other processes, such as softening and melting butter, melting chocolate and jelly, drying breadcrumbs and herbs, roasting nuts and more. Defrosting takes minutes instead of hours. Reheating is simple – with good results guaranteed if you follow a few straightforward rules (see page 43).

Ease of use
Controls are few and almost anyone can use them. They are simple and safe enough for the elderly or disabled, and even children. The dishes rarely get dangerously hot. Microwave ovens may be plugged in anywhere there is a 13 amp or 15 amp socket outlet. So they can be moved from room to room (perhaps on a trolley) or even outside.

Clean and cool
Oven cleaning is minimal and easy. The cavity walls are not heated up so splashes or spillages do not bake on – they are easily wiped away with a damp cloth. Similarly the kitchen remains cooler since the microwave oven itself does not heat up. There are fewer cooking smells with less steam. All these can be plus points if you wish to cook and eat (and perhaps live) in the same room.

Less washing up
Food can be cooked and/or reheated in the serving dish. Drinks can be heated in the mug or cup. Since there is no direct heat involved foods are not baked on.

Convenience and good results
Food can be prepared *when* it is required so there is less need to plan meals so far ahead.
   Foods cook in their own juices with flavours concentrated as a result – this is particularly noticeable when cooking vegetables and fish. Microwave cooking uses the minimum amount of water while cooking extremely quickly – ideal conditions to retain maximum amounts of vitamins and minerals. It is also most suitable for low-fat cooking – an important factor bearing in mind today's diet-conscious eating habits.

LIMITATIONS
Deep fat frying should *never* be attemped in a microwave oven.

Eggs in their shell cannot be cooked or reheated – they will explode.

Batter-coated foods do not reheat successfully – they become soggy. Fried and roast potatoes reheat with similar results.

Boiling more than 500ml/1pt water is more economically done in a kettle. Pies, pizzas, crusty bread, pancakes, Yorkshire pudding, meringues and soufflés all require conventional cooking.

Toasting bread is impossible in the microwave oven.

Heart pacemakers

Microwaves may affect certain types of pacemaker. A few early pacemakers *may* be susceptible to interference when in close proximity to electro-magnetic fields such as those caused by microwave ovens and some electric razors. If in doubt do not hesitate to seek medical advice.

Cling Film

Recent research (as yet not fully substantiated) suggests that the wrapping of food in some types of cling film may be harmful. Cling film has been on the market for over 30 years with no adverse effects, but if you are concerned about its safety there are alternative polythene wrappings available. In this book, cling film is recommended only as a cover for cooking food, for example over the top of a deep bowl where it does not actually touch the food itself. Remember always to pierce the cling film to allow steam to escape.

If your oven has an automatic temperature probe or sensor device, check with your instruction book on whether cling film may be used as a cover (or whether food may be covered at all), since covering could prevent the sensors from operating properly.

3

THE MICROWAVE OVEN

Conventional cooking methods rely on the application of heat to food by conduction, convection and radiation. In the microwave oven high frequency microwave energy is directed straight into the food. The resulting 'disturbance' of the food molecules causes heat to generate within it. It is this heat which cooks the food.

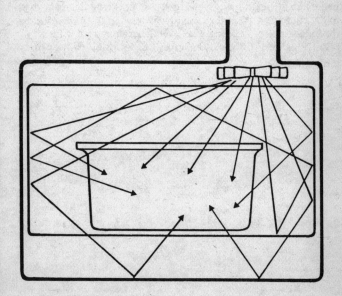

Fig. 1 Microwaves are spread around the oven cavity by a stirrer or paddle positioned at their entry point. They are *reflected* off all the inside walls as well as the roof and floor, whence they pass through the food container to be *absorbed* by the food. This book emphasises only placing food in the oven in suitable cookware (see page 26) through which microwaves pass easily. Metal containers must not be used as metal *reflects* the microwaves and may damage the oven.

Microwaves (electro-magnetic waves) are just as safe as radio or TV waves but are used differently. Here the microwave energy is being *absorbed* by food and liquids – in fact anything which contains water molecules – to make cooking possible.

Microwaves can also be *transmitted* i.e. they pass straight through materials, including glass, china, pottery, stoneware, plastics and paper. Thus these materials (which contain little or no water) may be used to hold food for cooking, defrosting and reheating in the microwave (see table on page 26).

Microwaves are *reflected* by metal. Microwaves are reflected off the inner surfaces of the oven cavity forming a wave pattern which ensures that the food receives energy from all directions. You will understand from this why metal food containers should not be used in the microwave oven. The waves which ought to be absorbed by the food would be deflected whenever the container got in the way – resulting in uneven and slower cooking and possible damage to the oven workings.

4

ADAPTING YOUR OWN RECIPES FOR MICROWAVE COOKING

Once you have mastered the art of microwave cooking (and cooked most types of food) you will know the quality of results which can be obtained, and those which you prefer. You will then wish to experiment with your own favourites. They will probably require some minor adaptations. Here are some checkpoints for guidance.

Find a similar recipe in your manufacturer's instruction book or in the pages which follow here, and use this as a basis for your method and cooking time. Use the ingredient with the longest cooking time as your guide to overall timing.

Cooking times will be shorter in the microwave oven. As a general rule allow one quarter to one third of the conventional time. For example, a dish which takes 40 minutes to cook conventionally will take about 12 minutes to cook by microwaves. There will be foods which do not fit into this rule so it is a good idea to underestimate times and check the dish often. Always allow for a *cooking*-standing time. Food will continue to cook after removal from the microwave oven, or when the energy is switched off. Heat is conducted from the hot outer areas to cooler central areas. The *cooking*-standing time actually helps complete the cooking process. The amount and density of food will dictate the *cooking*-standing time. Larger, denser foods require longer times. So you will see why it is preferable to under-cook foods prior to this standing time. Over-cooked food is spoilt but under-cooked food may always be cooked for a few minutes extra.

Most foods conventionally cooked by moist methods, e.g. boiling, steaming, poaching, and cooking in a liquid or sauce, are suitable for microwave cooking. Foods containing a large proportion of moisture cook well by microwave, e.g. soups, sauces, fruits, vegetables, poultry and fish. Casseroles are simply adapted to microwave cooking – if your oven has variable power, the cheaper less tender cuts of meat may be used with the entire cooking period on LOW, DEFROST or SIMMER. This slows down the cooking of casseroles. If it is extra speed you want, more tender (more expensive) cuts of meat may be substituted assuming economy allows. Alternatively you may find it more convenient to cook cheaper meat cuts conventionally, reheating (or defrosting and reheating) in the microwave oven.

Liquid quantities will probably need reducing by about 25% for microwave cooking. Since cooking times are much shorter there is less time for evaporation.

If necessary, extra liquid may be added towards the end of cooking.

Less fat may be needed in some recipes, e.g. cakes and biscuits. Follow your manufacturer's instruction book and similar recipes for guidance.

Cooking containers should be chosen with the view to serving in the same dish. No sticky saucepans to wash up.

Seasoning quantities should be reduced. Add strong flavours sparingly – they are concentrated in microwave cooking since less liquid is used. Check the seasoning before serving and adjust it if necessary. Do not season meat with salt before microwave cooking as this tends to dry out and toughen the surface. When brushing meat with butter to assist browning – use unsalted butter to avoid such toughening. Pepper, herbs and spices may be added during cooking. Add salt *after*.

Cake and pudding mixtures should fill the container to one third to half its depth only. They will rise quite dramatically during cooking.

Proper arrangement of food in the container, though not too important when cooking conventionally, produces more even defrosting, heating and cooking in the microwave oven. Thicker, denser foods should be arranged towards the outside of the dish with thinner, more porous foods towards its centre, e.g. small whole fish – heads to the outside, tails to the centre; chicken drumsticks or chops with thick ends to the outside. If possible arrange food leaving a space in the middle so larger areas of food are exposed to microwaves. Jacket potatoes, biscuits, small cakes, etc., should be arranged in a circle. Cakes are most successful when cooked in a ring mould.

Fig. 2 When reheating a plate of food arrange larger denser items towards the outer edge, smaller less dense ones to the middle (which tends to heat more slowly). For roasting, place bird/joint on a grid within a tray, so that the juices drip down and the meat is raised above them. Use a microwave thermometer to test the "doneness" of a joint or bird (put the thermometer in the *leg* of a chicken or turkey for correct readings). Remember to leave the thermometer in for up to 20 minutes after removal from the microwave oven.

The depth of foods should be even – spread food in the container rather than pile it up.

Some foods need re-arranging (moving about by stirring or turning over for example) to give even results. For instance, when reheating a dish of small whole potatoes a better result is obtained if, during cooking, those at the centre are moved to the outside, etc.

5

CHOOSING A
MICROWAVE OVEN

Choose a microwave oven with care – make sure that your chosen model will suit each of your particular requirements. Will it fit comfortably into your lifestyle? Do not forget to look ahead to the future. For example you may be just married but planning to have a family. The space available, ventilation requirements and the amount and type of other kitchen appliances you have will also dictate your choice of model. For example if you already have an efficient grill you are unlikely to need to buy a microwave oven with grill incorporated (remember it cannot be used during microwave cooking). Cost will be a major factor and it is worth doing your own survey. Prices vary considerably from model to model. Check that your chosen model holds the B.E.A.B. mark of safety or the "Approved For Safety" label from the Electricity Council. Check the guarantee – particularly for the magnetron. Does the manufacturer offer a service contract? Look at the instruction book – is it clear and comprehensive? Will the oven cavity be large enough for your needs – and containers? Are there indicator lights; is there a defrost control; or can you vary the power level? Assess the main types available.

Tabletop microwave ovens
These portable models are the most popular and fit neatly on the kitchen worktop. Some manufacturers have a specially designed (strong) trolley available for easy removal from room to room.

Two-level microwave ovens
This type has a removable shelf so that two layers of food can be microwaved at the same time. Microwave energy is usually directed via the sides of the cavity rather than the top. The food on the lower level (usually the floor of the oven) receives less microwave energy – so foods which require a shorter cooking period are positioned here. The overall cooking period of these ovens will be longer since

the microwave energy available has to be "shared" between a larger
amount of food.

Double-oven microwave cookers

These are available as free-standing cookers or as two-level built-in
appliances. (Usually the microwave oven is immediately above a
conventional oven. The grill is often inside the conventional oven
and the hob may sit above or separately.) Microwave and
conventional cooking methods complement each other with ease
and the accompanying instruction book usually offers structured
guidance. This way for example foods can be started off in the
microwave oven and browned or crisped in the adjacent
conventional oven (pies). Though the tabletop type can be used in
the same way, "double-oven" microwave cookers are worth
considering if you are refitting a kitchen.

Combination microwave cookers

These provide microwave and conventional cooking in the same
oven cavity – at a price. Microwave and conventional cooking can
take place separately, one after the other, or simultaneously. It is
possible to cook an entire meal in one oven (pre-setting the
microwave/conventional cooking periods) in a very short time –
producing a more traditionally cooked or baked result. Some
models offer simultaneous microwaving and grilling. The microwave power output of these ovens is a little lower than other types
but perhaps offers the last word in convenience.

Other features

Some models are more sophisticated than others and during your
survey you will be offered many "plus points", which may sound
confusing. So it is a good idea to browse through the list of
features below, decide which appeal to your specific needs and then
consider them (and the costs involved) when you are buying.

Turntable: These ensure even cooking, turning the food through
the microwave energy pattern in the cavity so that no hot and cold
spots occur. Stirring and hand-turning of food is therefore cut to a
minimum. They are made of toughened glass or glass ceramic and
begin to rotate as soon as the microwave energy is switched on.

Turntable alternative: In some ovens special hidden stirrers,
positioned usually in the roof or under the floor of the oven cavity,

distribute the microwave energy evenly through the oven. This produces a similar result to a turntable (without the food moving) and makes for easier cleaning.

Defrost control: The most basic microwave ovens now incorporate this defrosting facility. Often it is part of a variable power programme. The microwave power is reduced or is fed into the cavity in "bursts" so that defrosting areas of food are allowed to conduct their heat to adjacent frozen areas without themselves becoming too hot. In earlier models which may not have a defrost control the oven may be switched on and off manually to simulate the action. The defrost control can also be used for foods which conventionally require longer, slower cooking (casseroles for example).

Variable power: This facility enables the user to alter the speed with which the microwave energy enters the oven – to automatically control the rate of cooking. Levels may include high or full power, roast, bake, reheat, simmer, defrost, keep warm, low.

Browning dish: See page 30.

Browning grill/element: Positioned in the top of the microwave oven cavity, this is used to brown food before or after microwave cooking (not simultaneously). This is worth considering if you do not already have an efficient grill.

Temperature probe/sensor: This is particularly useful when cooking joints of meat. Microwave cooking is automatically controlled by the internal temperature of the food rather than by the cooking time. (See also page 30.)

Touch controls: Easy to clean.

Memory controls: These are a little more complicated and take a little more practice to use. They enable the user to pre-set microwave cooking power levels and times. For example the oven may be set to switch on at a certain time of the day (perhaps while you are out), to bring the food up to boil, then simmer for x amount of time and keep it warm until a pre-set time. Some models require "feeding in" of instruction cards. Some have touch control.

6

LOOKING AFTER YOUR MICROWAVE OVEN

Like most electrical appliances, the microwave oven will give you long and efficient service if it is properly looked after. Before trying out your new oven read the manufacturer's instructions carefully – familiarise yourself with them and always keep the book handy for speedy reference.

There is not much cleaning involved with a microwave oven. It provides a particularly clean method of cooking. The walls of the oven cavity do not heat up so foods do not bake on, and, since most foods are covered during cooking, defrosting or reheating, there is little spitting or splashing. It is a simple matter to wipe the oven interior with a damp cloth after each use. It is then ready for the next operation. Should splashing occur, the oven will lose some efficiency if food is left on the walls – microwave energy will concentrate on the splashed areas. So keep the inside nice and clean and cover foods if possible to minimise the need for cleaning.

Never use abrasives or steel wool when cleaning; scratching distorts the microwave pattern.

Do not operate the oven without food inside, since this can damage the magnetron. As a safeguard against switching on the oven accidentally even once, keep a small container of water in the oven.

Do not use metal containers in the microwave oven. Decorative metal designs on china or ovenware will blacken when exposed to microwaves. The microwave pattern is also distorted. Use foil only when recommended by your instruction book. Always remove twist ties.

Do not tamper with the oven cavity, door, casing or switches at any time. Always obtain qualified help if a fault occurs – do not attempt to repair it yourself. Check first, though, that the fuse in the plug has not blown before calling an engineer.

Have the oven serviced once a year by a manufacturer's authorised agent. Perhaps your manufacturer offers a home service contract.

WARNING: Do not slam the door, lean heavily on it or attempt to close it with anything between it and the oven front. Do not try to dry tea towels on it or use the oven to store utensils, etc. A perfect seal is required when the door is shut and the oven is working. Nothing must be done which might destroy the security of that seal and if you even suspect damage then have a qualified engineer to check it before further use.

Remove any lingering smells by boiling water and lemon in the oven at regular intervals during the week. They will soon disappear.

7

THE FREEZER

Freezing involves reducing the temperature of food to a level when chemical changes are slowed down and micro-organisms are inactivated. Food is frozen to and maintained at a temperature of — 18°C/0°F or lower to keep the food in the same condition as when it first entered the freezer. When the food is thawed or defrosted deterioration begins again. For this reason food which has been defrosted should not be refrozen. Raw food should always be cooked before refreezing, and defrosted cooked food should always be used at once (to avoid the possibility of food poisoning).

Freezing must be completed speedily. If food is frozen slowly, unduly large ice crystals are formed within the food. Foods with a high moisture content are the most affected. As the crystals expand during freezing they puncture the food cells. The cells then collapse during thawing, producing a poor (often discoloured) result.

The faster food is frozen the better its original condition is maintained. Fast freezing is usually controlled by a fast-freeze switch. When switched on it over-rides the thermostat causing the temperature to fall. It continues to fall as new food freezes. Meanwhile neither the temperature of the cabinet, nor the temperature of frozen food already in the freezer, rises. Some freezers have a separate compartment for fast freezing instead, so that new, warmer, food does not affect other areas. Follow your manufacturer's instructions for freezing food if you are to obtain best results when defrosting, reheating or cooking in the microwave oven.

Star ratings
One large white and three small dark stars on a freezer means it can freeze fresh food at a lower temperature than — 18°C/0°F, which is ideal for storing. Freezing areas in fridges have ratings which correspond to symbols on pre-packed frozen foods. Three stars indicate a temperature of — 18°C/0°F and a storage time of three months; two stars — 12°C/10°F, one month; and one star — 6°C/21°F, one week.

Whether you choose a chest or an upright freezer will depend mainly on where you intend to position it. A chest freezer is more economical to run, with more storage space, but it takes up a lot of floor space. An upright freezer or fridge/freezer is usually more suitable for the kitchen.

CHECKPOINTS FOR FREEZING

Use containers, dishes and plates suitable both for freezer *and* microwave. This way home-made food may be frozen, defrosted and then heated or cooked in the same container (ideal containers are listed on page 26). Wrap and seal the container securely, using freezer foil or a heavy duty freezer bag. If you wish to use the container while the food is in the freezer, line the dish with foil, pour in the food, freeze it, remove the food and wrap and label it before returning it to your freezer. To defrost; remove the wrapping, return the frozen block to its container, cover and defrost.

Cook extra portions of food, whether cooking conventionally or by microwave oven. Freeze them so that meals and snacks can be defrosted and then reheated in minutes.

Always remove foil wrappings and containers and twist ties before putting food in the microwave oven.

Freeze single portions to make the most of your microwave and freezer. An individual meal can then be ready in minutes without any food preparation. When I am away from home this is a great boon and very little extra effort is required by the cook. I know that my family are still eating filling, well-balanced meals.

For the same reasons, freeze small items (e.g. sausages, bacon rashers, chops, etc.) individually. They can then be packed and sealed in one large parcel but defrosted in whatever quantity may be required later. Some foods can be cut into individual portions prior to freezing – such as pies, pizzas, savoury and sweet flans, cakes. No need to defrost the whole dish, some of which might be wasted as a consequence.

Cool all foods completely before freezing and freeze covered (particularly plated meals).

8

EQUIPMENT TO USE

You will probably have in your cupboards many containers, dishes, bowls, plates, casseroles, and so on, suitable for microwave cooking, heating and defrosting. Similarly you may have plenty of types suitable for freezing and defrosting. When buying containers look for labels indicating their suitability for use in the microwave or in the freezer or both. Ask yourself too whether you will require them for serving as well as cooking, reheating or defrosting – the appearance could matter.

Freezer-to-microwave ovenware may be used for freezing down conventionally-cooked foods. These are fine for subsequent defrosting and then reheating in the microwave oven. They can also be used for prime cooking of foods such as vegetables, eggs, sauces, cakes, etc. They are made of high density polythene. Its temperature tolerance means that it may be used over and over again. However they are not suitable for use in high temperatures (i.e. in the conventional oven for example) and should not be exposed to direct heat (under a browning element or grill). Foods with high fat or sugar content should not be cooked in these containers – they will cause distortion of the plastic (for example, jam, syrup, sausages, bacon).

When used in the freezer, place the container of food inside a polythene freezer bag, extract as much air as possible, tie and label. For defrosting and/or reheating in the microwave oven, remove tie and bag. If a cover is needed – use kitchen paper.

The following table shows types of containers and materials which may also be used.

To test whether a container or utensil is suitable for cooking in the microwave oven:

Place the container in the microwave oven with a cup of water poured into it. Cook on HIGH for two minutes. After this time

Application

	Microwave cooking	Freezing	Microwave defrosting	Microwave reheating
Oven glass, e.g. Pyrex	Yes	Yes	Yes	Yes
Glass ceramic, e.g. Pyrosil	Yes	Yes	Yes	Yes
China/porcelain (not those with decorative metal borders)	No	No	Yes	Yes
Stoneware	Yes	Yes	Yes	Yes
Pottery (glazed only) (test for suitability first – see page 25)	Yes	No	No	Yes
Glass (not crystal)	No	No	No	Short term only
Ovenable board (semi-disposable dishes)	Yes	Yes	Yes	Yes
Basketware	No	No	No	Short term only
Cling film	Covering only	Heavy duty freezer film	Covering only	Covering only

Application

	Microwave cooking	Freezing	Microwave defrosting	Microwave reheating
Boil-in-bags (pierce before microwaving)	Yes	Yes	Yes	Yes
Freezer bags (120-200 gauge)	No	Yes	Yes	No
Roasting bags	Yes	No	No	Yes
Plastic (only use types specifically for use with boiling water – if they are dishwasher-safe they should be suitable for use in the microwave)	Some	Yes	Yes	Short term only – unless specifically designed for microwave use
Plastic foam cups and plates	No	No	Yes	Bread products only
Paper cups and plates	No	No	Yes	Yes
Paper towels, serviettes and doilies	Covering and absorbing moisture only	No	Covering and absorbing moisture only	Covering and absorbing moisture only

Do not use the following materials in the microwave oven: Metal and foil containers (some containers are lined with foil so take care); conventional oven thermometers.

(a) if the water is warm and the dish cool, it may be used; (b) if the dish is slightly warm it may still be used but food will take longer to cook in it; (c) if the water is cool and the dish is hot, it is *not suitable* for use – it has been absorbing the microwave energy.

Cooking containers: their shape and size

Good results will be obtained if you consider the shape and size of the container as well as the food you wish to cook in it.

The size should suit the amount of food. It will spill over if too full. Allow plenty of room for foods which tend to boil up during cooking. Too large a container used for a small amount of food will result in over-cooking as liquid areas spread over the base.

These diagrams will help you to understand how the shape of a container affects the cooking of the food inside it.

Circular

Microwaves have equal access to all sides of the food. The centre cooks more slowly than the outer edges.

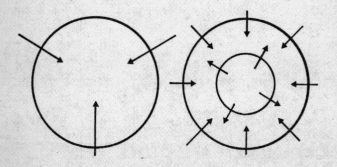

Ring

Microwaves have equal access to all sides but the slow-cooking centre has been removed.

Square

Microwaves have two directions in which to enter food at the corners which tend to over-cook. Extra stirring during cooking will assist heat distribution.

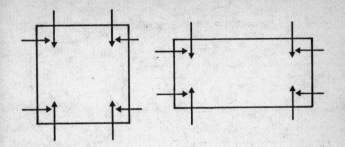

Oblong

Microwaves have two directions in which to enter food at the corners which, like in a square shape, tend to over-cook. Additionally this creates a slow-cooking centre. Extra stirring during cooking will assist heat distribution.

Straight sides

Microwaves enter top and bottom of food. Some over-cooking may occur at the corners. Extra stirring during cooking will help distribute the heat.

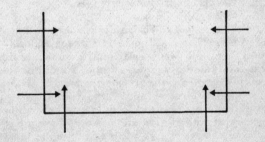

Slanted sides

Microwaves have extra access to food near the top edges. Extra stirring will help distribute the heat.

Bowl
There are no corners so microwaves enter the food more evenly.

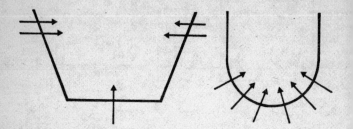

Useful extra microwave accessories
Several manufacturers offer extensive ranges of microwave accessories and cookware. Here are a few items I find useful – each specially designed for use in the microwave oven.

Roasting racks: These are made of tough plastic or a ceramic and raise meats and poultry above their accumulating cooking juices. They are also useful for reheating breads, pastry and other dry foods.

Plate rings: These are used for stacking plates when defrosting and/or reheating plated meals in the microwave oven. (Stack no more than two plates at a time for even results.)

Browning dishes or skillets: These are sometimes provided with the microwave oven. They should not be used in a conventional oven or on a conventional hob. Made of glass ceramic with a special coating on the base they absorb microwave energy. The dish is pre-heated in the microwave oven so that its base becomes hot. When food is placed on the dish it is seared and browns on contact. Microwave cooking is then carried out, the food being turned over half way through so that both/all sides are browned. These are ideal for bacon, chops, sausages, steaks, beefburgers, fish, chicken, toasted sandwiches, eggs, tomatoes, mushrooms – in fact most foods which are conventionally grilled or fried. Be guided by manufacturer's instructions for their use.

Microwave thermometers: Conventional thermometers can only be inserted in food *after* it has been removed from the microwave oven – microwaves affect the mercury. Thermometers designed for use in the microwave oven (while it is switched on) should be used following manufacturer's instructions. Some microwave models have a temperature sensing probe built into the oven cavity. The oven automatically switches off when the food, in which the probe is inserted, reaches the pre-set temperature.

9

A GUIDE TO DEFROSTING

Frozen food no longer takes hours to defrost. It takes minutes only, so there is no need to plan meals hours in advance of eating, and you can take meals in your stride when unexpected visitors arrive at the door – hungry.

Defrosting takes place faster with help from microwave energy. This energy, however, must be applied with care. The smallest ice crystals melt first and, if frozen food is subjected to a continuous period of microwave energy, the areas which have melted first begin to heat up while adjacent parts remain frozen. The result is most unsatisfactory with hot and frozen food in the same dish. Better results are obtained when the microwave energy is applied in short bursts with rests between. The periods of rest allow warmth from the defrosted food to be conducted to the frozen areas and ensure that the larger ice crystals also begin to melt.

Many microwave ovens incorporate a LOW or DEFROST setting which automatically switches the power on and off to ensure even thawing. This setting represents 30–50% of the oven's microwave energy: 200W–300W in a 600W–700W oven. If your microwave oven does not have a DEFROST setting you can still thaw frozen foods, though it will take a little longer and a little more effort. Turn the oven onto HIGH for 30 seconds, then off for 1½ minutes. Repeat this process until the food is defrosted. Rest periods for larger items such as meat joints and whole poultry should last at least twenty minutes. In this case, the DEFROST time on HIGH will also be longer – see page 36.

Some foods can be cooked directly from frozen. Vegetables are the best example (see chart on page 68). However, as explained below, most foods require a *defrosting*-standing time so that defrosting is complete before microwave cooking begins. Meat joints and poultry should always be *completely thawed* before cooking if good results are to be obtained.

After defrosting, food needs to "stand" before cooking or reheating. The warmth from those areas of food already thawed will ensure the melting of any remaining ice crystals nearby. The result will be an even defrosted temperature. Defrosting will continue after the microwave oven is switched off, so allow for this standing time. It is an integral part of the thawing process. Without this essential *defrosting*-standing time food may dry out on the edges, or start cooking.

Freezing food in suitable containers or dishes saves time and washing-up – there is no need to turn it out into another dish when it is defrosted. Check the chart on page 26 for the most versatile containers.

Cook extra portions, e.g. of a roast meal or casserole, and freeze ready for a quick, hearty meal on another day. One portion may often be frozen on the plate but you may find that several portions are best frozen in blocks (of meat in gravy, vegetables, etc.) and plated after defrosting.

CHECKPOINTS FOR DEFROSTING

Cover food during defrosting, except baked foods such as bread, cakes and pastry.

Use a dish or container which fits the frozen block of food as closely as possible so that thawed areas do not spread out and over-heat. It is a good idea to freeze food in the container in which it is to be defrosted and reheated. To avoid the container being out of use (in the freezer) for a long period, line it with foil before adding the food. Freeze it, remove the frozen block (you will need a straight-sided dish) and wrap it. Before defrosting simply peel off the foil and replace the frozen block in its dish.

Remove large lumps of ice from foods to be defrosted – vegetables and fruits for example. Extra ice will slow down the process.

Separate foods such as chops, sausages, etc., as they thaw – this produces a more even result, faster.

Open cartons before microwave defrosting, and pierce plastic covering or packaging – to allow for the expansion of air inside, and any steam build-up.

Remove metal ties from bags, replacing them with string.

Turn or rotate food during defrosting. This is done automatically if your oven has a turntable or stirrers. Large items such as joints of meat and whole poultry will require turning over at least once during defrosting to encourage even thawing. Legs and thin areas may be covered with foil pieces to prevent cooking. Check with your manufacturer's instruction books regarding the use of foil. It is essential to allow some *defrosting*-standing time before cooking (see chart, page 36) to allow the temperatures to equalise.

Use a food thermometer to indicate whether the centre of a meat joint has defrosted. Unless it is a special microwave oven food thermometer, do not leave it in the oven during defrosting or cooking.

Pour off liquid from meat and poultry which is being defrosted in its bag. The liquid slows down defrosting by absorbing the microwaves.

Finish defrosting poultry by immersing it in cold water during the *defrosting*-standing time. Defrosting completely in the microwave oven usually causes outer areas to begin to cook while the centre (the giblet bag) is still frozen. It is essential to *completely* defrost poultry and meat before cooking.

Break up foods such as liquids, soups, sauces and casseroles during defrosting. Use a fork or spoon and stir occasionally once defrosting has really started. Packages which do not allow for breaking up or stirring should be flexed to spread the heat – for example boil-in-bag. (Remember to pierce the bag to let out expanding air and steam).

Decant commercially frozen foods from their foil packages (since these reflect microwaves, thawing will be uneven) into suitable close-fitting containers before defrosting. Several frozen food manufacturers now give microwave instructions on the packet, so do check before discarding.

Place on kitchen paper food such as bread, cakes and pastries – to absorb the moisture.

Some foods do not need rest periods during defrosting. Small pieces of food such as left-overs, pastries, cakes, fish fillets and single bacon rashers can be subjected to a short continuous period of defrosting on HIGH.

Food frozen at home usually takes longer to defrost than commercially frozen food. The ice crystals tend to be larger and require more energy to thaw.

When plating meals for the freezer, make sure that the food lies within the edge of the plate. Do not overlap food. Thicker, denser items should be arranged towards the outer edge.

Defrosting times will vary according to the food's shape, weight and density and its storage temperature in the freezer. Your instruction book will give you details for your particular model. Remember it is always preferable to *underestimate* defrosting times. If the food is not completely thawed after the *defrosting*-standing time then it may simply be returned to the microwave oven for a short time longer (allow a short time for standing too).

The table below may be used as an approximate guide to defrosting times.

DEFROST GUIDE

Times may vary according to the density and frozen temperature of the food, and the power of your microwave oven. When increasing or decreasing quantities alter the defrosting times accordingly. Check the food regularly – twice as much food does not necessarily mean twice the defrost time.

Food	Weight/size/no.	Time on LOW/ DEFROST setting	Defrosting-standing time	Hints
FISH *Note: Some fish are better defrosted in two stages, each consisting of a few minutes on LOW or DEFROST followed by some defrosting-standing time. This is indicated below by two groups of timings being given.*				
White fish fillets/ Cutlets, e.g. cod, coley, haddock, halibut, plaice, sole, turbot, hake, skate.	450 g / 1 lb	3–4 minutes + 2–3 minutes	5 minutes 5 minutes	Cover during defrosting, drain off excess water, and dry before cooking.
Oily fish (whole) e.g. herring, mackerel, trout, salmon (cutlets)	225 g / 8 oz	2–3 minutes + 3–4 minutes	5 minutes 5 minutes	Ditto
Kipper fillets	225 g / 8 oz	2–3 minutes	2 minutes	Ditto
Prawns, shrimps, scampi, crabmeat.	225 g / 8 oz	3–4 minutes	5 minutes	Ditto
Prawns etc.	100 g / 4 oz	2½ minutes	2 minutes	Ditto

Food	Weight/size/no.	Time on LOW/DEFROST setting	Defrosting-standing time	Hints
Lobster tails	225 g/8 oz	3–4 minutes + 2–3 minutes	5 minutes 5 minutes	Ditto
Fish casserole	To serve 4	16–18 minutes	10 minutes	Cover during defrosting
Boil-in-the-bag fish in sauce	150 g/5 oz	3½–5 minutes	2 minutes	Pierce bag before defrosting
Boil-in-bag prawn curry	175 g/6 oz	5–6 minutes	2 minutes	Ditto

MEAT

Always place meat in a shallow dish during defrosting – to catch the juices. Remember to "rest" joints, and turn them over, during defrosting to produce an even result (you will not want the joint to cook in one area while another is still frozen – see page 32).

Beef				
Boneless joints	per 450 g/1 lb	8–10 minutes	20 minutes – 1 hour	Cover during defrosting
Joints with bone	per 450 g/1 lb	10–12 minutes	20 minutes – 1 hour	Ditto
Minced beef	450 g/1 lb	8–10 minutes	10 minutes	Cover during defrosting and break up with a fork during defrosting.
Steak	450 g/1 lb	8–10 minutes	10 minutes	Cover during defrosting.

Food	Weight/size/no.	Time on LOW/DEFROST setting	Defrosting-standing time	Hints
Veal				
Joints (boned)	per 450 g/1 lb	7–8 minutes	20–45 minutes	Cover during defrosting.
Escalopes	450 g/1 lb	6–7 minutes	10 minutes	Separate during defrosting.
Lamb				
Joints	per 450 g/1 lb	5–8 minutes	20–45 minutes	Cover narrow ends with foil.
Chops	450 g/1 lb	6–10 minutes	10–15 minutes	Separate during defrosting.
Spare ribs	450 g/1 lb	5–8 minutes	10 minutes	Ditto
Minced lamb	450 g/1 lb	8–10 minutes	10 minutes	Break up with a fork during defrosting.
Pork				
Always make sure pork is *completely* defrosted before cooking.				
Joints	per 450 g/1 lb	8 minutes	30 minutes – 1 hour	Cover bone ends with foil.
Chops	450 g/1 lb	6–10 minutes	10–15 minutes	Separate during defrosting.
Spare ribs	450 g/1 lb	6–8 minutes	10 minutes	Ditto
Sausages	450 g/1 lb	6 minutes	10–15 minutes	Ditto

Food	Weight/size/no.	Time on LOW/ DEFROST setting	Defrosting- standing time	Hints
Bacon See times for **PORK** when defrosting joints and chops.				
Rashers	225 g / 8 oz	1½–2 minutes	5–8 minutes	Separate rashers before standing time.
Offal Liver (lamb/pig/ calf/ox)	450 g / 1 lb	8–10 minutes	5 minutes	Separate pieces during defrosting.
Kidney (lamb/pig/ calf/ox)	450 g / 1 lb	6–10 minutes	5 minutes	Ditto

POULTRY

Always make sure poultry is *completely* defrosted before cooking. Whole poultry may be defrosted in its original plastic wrapping (remove any metal ties). Stand the bird in cold water during *defrosting*-standing time (see page 34). With variable power microwave ovens whole birds may be more quickly defrosted by using two power levels. So defrosting is reduced to about 35 minutes followed by a 20-30 minute *defrosting*-standing time. Check with your instruction book.

Food	Weight/size/no.	Time on LOW/ DEFROST setting	Defrosting- standing time	Hints
Chicken/duck, whole	per 450 g / 1 lb	6–8 minutes	30 minutes	Standing the bird in cold water will speed up defrosting and assist in the removal of giblets.
Turkey, whole	per 450 g / 1 lb	1 minute breast side up 30 seconds breast side down	30 minutes 2–3 hours	Ditto
Chicken/turkey portions	per 450 g / 1 lb	7 minutes	5–10 minutes	Separate during defrosting.

Food	Weight/size/no.	Time on LOW/ DEFROST setting	Defrosting-standing time	Hints
VEGETABLES Can be cooked from frozen. Cooking times on page 68				
RICE Cooked	225 g/8 oz	2 minutes	5 minutes	Break up with fork during defrosting.
FRUIT Soft fruit, sliced apples, melon balls, etc.	225 g/8 oz 450 g/1 lb	3–4 minutes 4–6 minutes	10–30 minutes	Allow to stand until thawed completely. Stir or shake *gently* during defrosting.
Fruit juice concentrate	178 ml/6¼ fl oz	2–3 minutes	3–5 minutes	Remove any metal from carton and break up and stir during defrosting.
DESSERTS Cheesecake with fruit topping	Family size	2½–4 minutes	20 minutes	Place on serving dish before standing.
Fruit crumble	Family size	12 minutes	10 minutes	
Fruit pie	Family size Individual	3–4 minutes 1 minute	10 minutes 2 minutes	
Trifle	Individual	1 minute	15 minutes	Remove lid before defrosting.
Mousse	Individual	30 seconds	15 minutes	Ditto

Food	Weight/size/no.	Time on LOW/DEFROST setting	Defrosting-standing time	Hints
PASTRY and pastry dishes				
Shortcrust/puff	225 g/8 oz	1 minute	15–20 minutes	Remove any foil wrapper, and wrap loosely in kitchen paper.
	395 g/14 oz	2 minutes	20–30 minutes	
Quiche or savoury flan	Family size	3–5 minutes	5 minutes	
Meat pie	Family size	7 minutes	10 minutes	
Danish pastry	150 g/5 oz	1½ minutes	5 minutes	
Apple strudel	One	45 seconds	5 minutes	
Fruit pie – see Desserts	One	30 seconds	5 minutes	
CAKES				
Sponge cake	Family size	1½–2 minutes	5–10 minutes	Place on kitchen paper, turn over after 1 minute.
Cream sponge cake	Family size	1½ minutes or 30 seconds on HIGH	20–30 minutes	Ditto
Small cakes	Four	1–1½ minutes	5 minutes	Place on kitchen paper.
Scones	Four	1½ minutes	5 minutes	Ditto
Jam doughnuts	Four	1½–2½ minutes	5 minutes	Place on kitchen paper. Take care – if eaten immediately the jam may be very hot.
Cream doughnuts	Four	1¼–1¼ minutes	10 minutes	Place on kitchen paper.
Cream éclairs	Four	1–1½ minutes	15–20 minutes	Ditto

Food	Weight/size/no.	Time on LOW/DEFROST setting	Defrosting-standing time	Hints
BREAD				
Loaf, whole	Large	6-8 minutes	10-15 minutes	Unwrap and place on kitchen paper. Turn over during defrosting.
	Small	4-6 minutes	5-10 minutes	
Loaf, sliced	Large	6-8 minutes	10-15 minutes	Remove any metal ties and defrost in wrapper.
	Small	4-6 minutes	5-10 minutes	
Bread slice	One	10-15 seconds	1-2 minutes	Place on kitchen paper.
Bread rolls	Two	15-20 seconds	2-3 minutes	Ditto
	Four	15-20 seconds	2-3 minutes	Ditto
Croissants	Four	30-45 seconds	2 minutes	Ditto
OTHER ITEMS				
Sauce, sweet or savoury	550 ml/1 pt	10-12 minutes	10 minutes	Break up and stir during defrosting.
	300 ml/½ pt	6-8 minutes	5-10 minutes	Cover during defrosting.
Plated meal	350 g/12 oz	3-4 minutes	2 minutes	
Faggots in gravy	4-pack	5-7 minutes	10 minutes	Remove from foil container; cover.
Soup	550 ml/1 pt	8-12 minutes	10 minutes	Break up and stir during defrosting
Pizza	Family size	3-4 minutes	5 minutes	Place on kitchen paper.
Lasagne	Family size	15 minutes	10 minutes	
Shepherds pie	Family size	8-10 minutes	10 minutes	
Butter/margarine	250 g/8.82 oz.	1½-2 minutes	5 minutes	Remove any foil wrappers.
Cream	300 ml/½ pt	1-2 minutes	10-15 minutes	Remove any metal lids.
Cream cheese	75 g/3 oz	1-1½ minutes	10-15 minutes	Remove any foil wrappers.

Other cheese - very difficult to defrost, best done ordinarily (cheddar, etc.).

10

A GUIDE TO REHEATING

Reheating foods is simple with your microwave oven. Most foods reheat without loss of colour, quality or flavour, and you will find you waste less food and fuel too. Meals prepared in advance may be reheated later, by a family member home late, with no need to heat up the entire conventional oven. Additionally reheating in the microwave is far more successful and tasty than conventional methods. There is little or no drying up of food edges and the speed of reheating gives harmful germs less chance to survive. In fact the food will be as appealing and flavourful as when it was first prepared.

REHEATING CHECKPOINTS

Reheating times will depend on the starting temperature of the food. Food taken from the fridge will take longer than that at room temperature. Frozen food will take longer since it may require a period for defrosting first, followed by a *defrosting*-standing time (when the heat from the melted ice crystals is conducted to the frozen areas to continue the defrosting process). See chart on page 36. A plated meal requires 3-4 minutes to reheat from room temperature.

Overheating dries and toughens foods. It is better to *underestimate* times and return the food to the oven for another few seconds/minutes. At first you will be surprised how quickly some foods reheat, e.g. bread and small cakes, pastries and rolls. Follow manufacturers' instructions and generally practise. This way you will perfect reheating times. Wrapping starchy foods, such as jacket potatoes, in polythene prevents them from drying out. When reheating mashed potato make a hollow in the centre and add a knob of butter.

Don't be deceived by the 'warm' temperature of the pastry of small pies – the inside will be very *hot* and they should be allowed to stand for a short period after coming out of the microwave oven for the heat to stabilise.

Cover foods well during reheating. Always pierce cling film to allow steam to escape. Cover plated metals with another plate.

Arrange foods on a plate in an even layer, with thicker, denser foods near the outer edge (see page 16).
   The food is reheated sufficiently when the centre bottom of the plate feels warm – heat will have been conducted there from the food. Use a stacking ring to heat two plated meals (but do not try to reheat three at once – the middle one will not reheat successfully). Increase the time by 50 per cent.

Stir soups, casseroles, sauces and other liquids to spread the heat evenly through. This will speed up reheating. Stir on removal from the oven too.

Turn food which cannot be stirred. Particularly if your oven does not have a turntable or special stirrers.

Take care when reheating vegetables without a sauce. Reheat gently on a low setting if possible to maintain the texture and to prevent toughening of fibres. Cover with a lid.

Absorb the moisture when reheating bread and bread products by standing them on kitchen paper. Wrap or cover pastry and pastry dishes with kitchen paper.

Cut meat into thin slices – they will reheat more evenly. Reheating meat slices in a gravy or sauce will prevent them from drying out.

Canned foods should be transferred to a suitable dish or container and covered during reheating.

Baby foods and drinks are reheated hygienically in their serving container, or bottle. Always stir well and *test for the correct temperature before serving.* Remember foods become very hot very quickly – particularly small amounts.

11

ABOUT THE RECIPES

The recipes in the following pages were developed using a microwave oven which has a variable power output up to 650W and a fitted turntable. For convenience when using most models cooking takes place on HIGH (or FULL power). Owners of variable power ovens will, with experience, wish to adapt the power levels to suit their own preferences. LOW or DEFROST setting is used to defrost foods.

You may find that cooking times will vary slightly according to the power output of your oven. The higher the wattage, the speedier the cooking will be.

Here is a guide to average cooking times in ovens of different outputs:

600–700W	500–600W	400–500W
30 seconds	35 seconds	40 seconds
1 minute	1 minute 10 seconds	1 minute 20 seconds
5 minutes	5 minutes 45 seconds	6 minutes 45 seconds
10 minutes	11 minutes 30 seconds	13 minutes 30 seconds
20 minutes	23 minutes	27 minutes
30 minutes	34 minutes 30 seconds	40 minutes 30 seconds

Always read and follow your manufacturer's instructions.

When in doubt about cooking times it is advisable to *under-estimate*. It is a simple matter to replace the food in the oven to cook for a little longer, and is preferable to over-cooking.

Cooking times will also vary according to the starting temperature of the food, its density, thickness, quality and quantity, and the type, shape and size of the container used. Your personal preferences will of course also affect cooking times and methods.

All cooking in the recipes takes place in the microwave oven unless specified. Freezing, defrosting and reheating instructions are given when appropriate, along with suitable *cooking*-standing times and *defrosting*-standing times.

Check with your instruction book regarding the need to turn food during cooking. If your oven has a built-in turntable or stirrers, there is no additional need to turn food in the recipes to come.

Recipe ingredients are given in metric, imperial and American quantities. It is advisable to follow one type of measure. Where accuracy is important exact equivalents are given – otherwise, figures have been rounded off to convenient measures. Ingredients are listed in their order of use for your convenience.

Before freezing all food should be *cooled completely*.

Each recipe begins with a detailed list as follows:

1. *Serves* –   Number of portions.
2. *Freezer life* –   Maximum recommended storage time in the freezer.
3. *Cook* –   Length of time for cooking in the microwave oven (and the appropriate setting) plus any extra browning or frying time.
4. *Cooking*-standing time The recommended time for this recipe to continue cooking after the microwave power is switched off.
5. *Defrost* –   Time taken on DEFROST setting in the microwave oven.
6. *Defrosting*-standing time –   The recommended time for this recipe to continue defrosting after switching off the microwave energy.
7. *Reheat* –   Recommended time and setting to reheat the finished recipe for serving.

When planning your meals simply check through these points to assess the suitability of a recipe for your needs and the preparation time available. Add up the times as appropriate to estimate the amount of cooking/preparation time.

12

CONVERSION TABLES

These are not exact, but 'rounded up'. When following recipes, always keep to the same set of measures (whether imperial, metric or American), never try to change in the middle from one to the other.

Capacities

1 fl oz	25 ml
2 fl oz	50 ml
¼ pt (5 fl oz)	150 ml
½ pt (10 fl oz)	300 ml
¾ pt (15 fl oz)	400 ml
1 pt (20 fl oz)	500–600 ml

Spoon Capacities
This refers to level spoons in each case.

¼ tsp	half 2.5 ml sp
½ tsp	2.5 ml sp
1 tsp	5 ml sp
2 tsp	10 ml sp
1 tbsp	15 ml sp

Weights

1 oz	25 g
2 oz	50 g
3 oz	75 g
4 oz	100–125 g
5 oz	150 g
6 oz	175 g
7 oz	200 g
8 oz	225 g
9 oz	250 g
10 oz	275 g
11 oz	300 g

12 oz	350 g	
13 oz	375 g	
14 oz	400 g	
15 oz	425 g	
16 oz (1 lb)	450 g	
1½ lb	700 g	
2 lb	900 g	

When a recipe refers to a can of food, check that you use the size specified, as cans vary tremendously. Where imperial/metric conversions are given on can labels, they are exact and are not rounded up or down as are the tables above.

American measures
Dry measures

Butter, margarine	1 lb/450 g	2 cups
	1 oz/25 g	2 tbsp
Flour	1 lb/450 g	4 cups
	1 oz/25 g	¼ cup
Sugar	1 lb/450 g	2 cups
	1 oz/25 g	2 tbsp
Dried fruit	1 lb/450 g	3 cups
Rice	1 lb/450 g	2 cups

Liquid measures
(Water, stock, milk, cooking oil, etc.)

	Am
¼ pt/150 ml	⅔ cup
½ pt/300 ml	1¼ cups
1 pt/550 ml	2½ cups

An imperial pint measures 20 fluid ounces, while an American pint measures 16 fluid ounces.

13

RECIPES

SOUPS AND STARTERS

Home-made soup can be a welcoming start to a meal, a warming snack, or a hearty meal in itself. They are prepared simply and speedily in the microwave oven to serve immediately, or to refrigerate and reheat, or to freeze, defrost and reheat.

Points for microwaving soups
Cook the soup in its tureen or serving dish (see the chart of suitable materials on page 26). It saves washing up if you reheat in the serving dish too.

Individual portions of soup are economically prepared in minutes.

Always use a container larger than required to allow the soup to bubble up during cooking – particularly milk-based soups.

Soups containing barley or lentils will require just as long as conventionally cooked soups.

Canned soup
Pour the canned soup into a serving tureen or bowl or into a jug or

individual soup bowls, if necessary diluting soup according to the
instructions on the label. Cover with a lid or cling film (remember
to pierce it to allow steam to escape). Cook on HIGH until hot. A
435g/ 15 oz can will need 3–4 minutes. Stir halfway through
cooking and again after removal from the oven. Allow a few
minutes *cooking*-standing time before serving (the soup should be
covered during this time).

Dried Soup Mixes   •
Make up the soup in a large serving tureen or bowl, or jug. It should
be two-thirds full only to allow the cooking soup to bubble up. Mix
the soup powder with 150ml/ ¼ pt of the recommended quantity of
water. Stir into a smooth paste and add the rest of the water (which
should be boiling). Cover and cook on HIGH for 8–10 minutes. Stir
once during cooking and once after removal from the microwave
oven. Allow 5 minutes *cooking*-standing time before serving.

   Soup mixes containing noodles or rice should be soaking in their
water for 20–30 minutes before cooking.

PARSNIP AND LEEK SOUP

A thick, delicately-flavoured soup. A meal in itself with crusty
bread and cheese.

Serves: 4   *Freezer life: 3 months*

Cook: 10 mins. + 3–5 mins. *Cooking*-standing time: Nil.
Defrost: 12 mins. *Defrosting*-standing time: 10 mins.
Reheat: 10 mins.

	Met.	*Imp.*	*Am.*
Parsnips, finely chopped or grated	**225g**	**8 oz**	**½ lb**
Leeks, finely sliced	**225g**	**8 oz**	**½ lb**
Chicken stock cube	**1**	**1**	**1**
Ground mace	**pinch**	**pinch**	**pinch**
Water	**150ml**	**¼ pt**	**⅔ cup**
Salt and ground black pepper			
Milk	**400ml**	**¾ pt**	**2 cups**
Chives, chopped	**15ml sp**	**1 tbsp**	**1 tbsp**

Method
Place all ingredients, except milk and chives, in a suitable container or casserole dish and stir well. Cover and cook on HIGH for 10 minutes (stirring well after 5 minutes). Stir in the milk and purée in a blender or through a sieve.

To serve: reheat on HIGH for 3–5 minutes. Sprinkle chives over.
To freeze: omit chives, pour into rigid polythene or microwave-freezer container, cool completely and freeze.
Defrost in same container, uncovered, for 12 minutes, breaking it up with a fork and stirring occasionally. Allow 10 minutes for *defrosting*-standing time then reheat for 10 minutes. •

CREAMY THICK TOMATO SOUP

Over-ripe tomatoes can be used and give a richer colour. No need to skin the tomatoes.

Serves: 6   *Freezer life: 3 months*

Cook: 14 mins + 5 mins. *Cooking*-standing time: Nil.
Defrost: 10 mins. *Defrosting*-standing time: 10 mins.
Reheat: 10 mins.

	Met.	Imp.	Am.
Tomatoes, quartered	450g	1 lb	1 lb
Potato, finely chopped	1 large	1 large	1 large
Leeks, finely sliced	2	2	2
Carrot (optional), finely sliced	1	1	1
Chicken stock	750ml	1¼ pt	3 cups
Worcestershire sauce	5 ml sp	1 tsp	1 tsp
Salt and ground white pepper			
Tomato purée or paste	3 × 15 ml sp	3 tbsp	3 tbsp
Single or thin cream	4 × 15 ml sp	4 tbsp	4 tbsp

Method
Place tomatoes, potatoes, leeks, carrot (optional), some of the stock (150ml/¼ pt/⅔ cup), the Worcestershire sauce and the seasoning into a suitable container or casserole. Cover and cook on

HIGH for 14 minutes (stirring after 7 minutes). Stir in the remaining cold stock and tomato purée. Purée the soup in a blender then pass through a sieve. Discard skins and seeds.

To serve: reheat on full for 5 minutes. Stir in cream just before serving. Do not boil once the cream has been added.
To freeze: pour into a rigid polythene or microwave-freezer container, cool completely and freeze.
Defrost in same container, uncovered, for 10 minutes, breaking it up with a fork and stirring occasionally. Then allow 10 minutes *defrosting*-standing time before reheating for 10 minutes.

MUSHROOM AND ONION SOUP

This is French onion soup with a difference.

Serves: 4–6   *Freezer life: 3 months*

Cook: 5 minutes + 10 minutes. *Cooking*-standing time: 10 minutes.
Defrost: 10 minutes. *Defrosting*-standing time: 10 minutes.
Reheat: 4–6 minutes.

	Met.	Imp.	Am.
Butter	50g	2 oz	4 tbsp
Onions, thinly sliced	450g	1 lb	1 lb
Beef stock, hot	550ml	1 pt	2½ cups
Worcestershire sauce	15ml sp	1 tbsp	1 tbsp
French mustard	2 × 5ml sp	2 tsp	2 tsp
Mushrooms, finely chopped	125 g	4 oz	¼ lb
Salt and pepper			

Method
In a suitable container, cook the butter and onions (covered) for 5 minutes on HIGH. Stir in the remaining ingredients, cover and cook on HIGH for 10 minutes, stirring once or twice during cooking. Allow a 10 minute *cooking*-standing time before serving.

Serve: With French bread and cheese.
To freeze: Cool completely and freeze in a suitable container.
Defrost for about 10 minutes followed by a 10 minute *defrosting*-standing time. Reheat on HIGH for 4–6 minutes.

FREEZER VEGETABLE SOUP

This recipe is ideal for using up small amounts of vegetables left in the freezer. The bacon gives it an interesting flavour.

Serves:4–6   *Freezer life: 3 months*

Cook: Onion and bacon 5 minutes, soup 25 minutes. *Cooking*-standing time: 10 minutes.
Defrost: 10 minutes. *Defrosting*-standing time: 10 minutes.
Reheat: 4–6 minutes.

	Met.	Imp.	Am.
Onion, chopped	1 medium	1 medium	1 medium
Streaky bacon rashers, chopped	4	4	4
Butter or margarine	15g	½ oz	1 tbsp
Chicken stock	800ml	1½ pts	3¾ cups
Potato, thinly sliced	1 medium	1 medium	1 medium
Tomato purée or paste	3 × 15ml sp	3 tbsp	3 tbsp
Mixed herbs	¼ × 5ml sp	¼ tsp	¼ tsp
Mixture of frozen vegetables	225g	8 oz	½ lb
e.g. beans, peas, sweetcorn, mushrooms, carrots, cauliflower			
Salt and pepper			

Method
Place onion, bacon and butter into a large suitable container, cover and cook on HIGH for 5 minutes. Add the remaining ingredients, including the frozen vegetables, cover and cook on HIGH for a further 25 minutes. Allow a *cooking*-standing time of 10 minutes before adjusting seasoning if necessary.

Serve: Sprinkled with Parmesan cheese.
To freeze: Cool completely and freeze in a rigid polythene or microwave-freezer container.
Defrost for 10 minutes and allow a further 10 minutes *defrosting*-standing time. Reheat on HIGH for 4–6 minutes.

CHINESE CHICKEN SOUP

This basic soup has an oriental flavour.

Serves: 4-6   *Freezer life: 3 months*

Cook: 3 minutes + 5 minutes + 10 minutes. *Cooking*-standing
time: 10 minutes.
Defrost: 10 minutes. *Defrosting*-standing time: 10 minutes.
Reheat: 4-6 minutes.

	Met.	Imp.	Am.
Chicken pieces (uncooked), thinly sliced	175g	6 oz	¼-½ lb
Spring onions, chopped	4	4	4
Butter	25g	1 oz	2 tbsp
Back bacon slices, chopped	1	1	1
Chicken stock, hot	1.2 l	2 pts	5 cups
Button mushrooms, quartered	125g	4 oz	¼ lb
Bean sprouts	125g	4 oz	¼ lb
Mixed herbs	pinch	pinch	pinch
Soy sauce	5ml sp	1 tsp	1 tsp
Salt and white pepper			

Method
Defrost the chicken pieces if necessary for 2-3 minutes and allow a
10 minute *defrosting*-standing time.

Place the spring onions, butter and bacon in a suitable large
container, cover and cook on HIGH for 3 minutes. Add the chicken
and cook, covered, on HIGH for 5 minutes. Add the remaining
ingredients, cover again and cook for a further 10 minutes on
HIGH. Allow a *cooking*-standing time of 10 minutes before
adjusting the seasoning if necessary.

Serve: Sprinkled with extra spring onion, freshly chopped.
To freeze: Cool completely in a rigid polythene or microwave-
freezer container and freeze.
To defrost: Microwave on DEFROST for 10 minutes and allow a
10 minute *defrosting*-standing time. Reheat on HIGH for 4-6
minutes.

BRANDIED LAMBS' LIVER PÂTÉ

An economical and impressive starter.

Serves: 4   *Freezer life: 2 months*

Cook: Butter/onion 1 minute, liver 3 minutes. *Cooking*-standing time: Nil.
Defrost: 2 minutes. *Defrosting*-standing time: 20 minutes plus.
Reheat: Not necessary.

	Met.	*Imp.*	*Am.*
Lamb's liver	225g	8 oz	½ lb
Red wine	2 × 15ml sp	2 tbsp	2 tbsp
Salt	½ × 5ml sp	½ tsp	½ tsp
Black pepper	¼ × 5ml sp	¼ tsp	¼ tsp
Cinnamon	pinch	pinch	pinch
Nutmeg	pinch	pinch	pinch
Spring onions, chopped	2	2	2
Butter	225g	8 oz	1 cup
Brandy	2 × 15ml sp	2 tbsp	2 tbsp
Lemon slices	to garnish		
Watercress			

Method
Defrost the liver if necessary for about 5–8 minutes and allow a *defrosting*-standing time of 5 minutes.

Wash the liver in cold water and remove any skin and membrane. Dry it with a paper towel and slice thinly. Put the wine and the four seasonings and the spring onions in a suitable container and cook uncovered on HIGH for 1 minute. Add the liver, stir well, cover and cook on HIGH for 3 minutes (or until the liver is cooked) stirring once or twice during cooking. Blend or liquidise the entire mixture with the butter and brandy (the butter may need softening for 30–45 seconds). Pour the pâté into four small dishes and chill for several hours.

To serve: Garnish with lemon slices and watercress and serve with crusty bread or toast.
To freeze: Cool completely, cover and freeze.
Defrost: On DEFROST for about 2 minutes. Take care not to allow the edges of the pâté to heat up. Allow a *defrosting*-standing time of at least 20 minutes.

CREAMY KIPPER APPETISER

This is a light but flavourful starter. Smoked mackerel may also be used in this recipe.

Serves: 4   *Freezer life: 1 month*

Cook: 2–3 minutes, butter 45–60 seconds. *Cooking*-standing time: Nil.
Defrost: 2 minutes. *Defrosting*-standing time: 10 minutes plus.
Reheat: Not necessary.

	Met.	Imp.	Am.
Kipper fillets	225g	8 oz	½ lb
Butter	50g	2 oz	4 tbsp
Double or thick cream	3 × 15ml sp	3 tbsp	3 tbsp
Lemon juice	15ml sp	1 tbsp	1 tbsp
Horseradish sauce	5ml sp	1 tsp	1 tsp
Salt and black pepper			

Method
DEFROST the kipper fillets if necessary for 2–3 minutes. Allow a 2 minute *defrosting*-standing time.

Place the kippers in a suitable container (or slit the bag if pre-packed), cover and cook on HIGH for 2–3 minutes, or until the kippers are cooked. Melt the butter in a small container on HIGH for 45–60 seconds. Blend or liquidise the kippers together with the remaining ingredients (add salt carefully – the kippers may be salty enough for your taste). Cool and chill before serving.

Serve: On a bed of lettuce with diced cucumber.
To freeze: Cool completely in a suitable container and freeze.
Defrost for about 2 minutes (make sure the mixture does not begin to heat up). Allow a *defrosting*-standing time of at least 10 minutes.

FISH

Fish may be cooked from fresh or frozen, in a microwave oven. You can also freeze cooked fish dishes to be defrosted and reheated later. Fresh or pre-cooked, frozen, tinned or boil-in-the-bag, the times are short. Not only is the finest flavour of the fish retained but in a microwave oven it keeps its shape perfectly (particularly a whole fish).

Clean and prepare fish in the normal way before microwave cooking. It is better to freeze fish in individual portions for easy-to-serve, substantial meals.

Points for microwaving fish

Overlap fish tails or thinner ends to help even cooking. Always cover fish. Remember to pierce cling film to allow steam to escape. Boil-in-bags should be pierced before cooking.

Always adjust seasoning *after* cooking.

When you cook fish with the skin intact, brush it with melted butter or oil before cooking. Slit the skin in two or three places to prevent it bursting. When cooking fish in a sauce, use DEFROST or a LOW power setting and use a longer cooking time (50% longer).

To disperse 'fishy' odours – boil a little water and lemon juice/vinegar in the microwave oven for 2-3 minutes.

Reheating fish (except after defrosting a prepared dish) should be avoided. It is easy to overcook and then the fish becomes tough and dry.

Fish fingers, breadcrumbed and battered fish can be cooked in the microwave oven but the results will not be crisp and golden.

As a general guide to cooking fresh fish, cooking times are as follows. Allow a *cooking*-standing time of 5 minutes.

Whole fish: 4–5 minutes per 450g / 1 lb on HIGH.

Fillets and steaks: 5–6 minutes per 450g / 1 lb on HIGH.

SMOKED FISH IN SHELLS

Four shells fit into the microwave oven at one time. A useful starter or snack which can also be prepared in advance and frozen.

Serves: 4   *Freezer life: 1 month*

Cook: Fish 2 mins, sauce 5 mins + 5 mins + browning under a conventional grill. *Cooking*-standing time: takes place under grill.
Defrost: 7 mins. *Defrosting*-standing time: 5 mins.
Reheat: 3 mins + browning under grill.

	Met.	Imp.	Am.
Smoked cod or haddock	600g	1¼ lb	1¼ lb
Lemon juice	15ml sp	1 tbsp	1 tbsp
Butter			
Black pepper			
Extra milk			
Milk	300ml	½ pt	1¼ cups
Bay leaf	1	1	1
Black peppercorns	6	6	6
Cloves	2	2	2
Onion, quartered	1 medium	1 medium	1 medium
Cornflour or cornstarch	2×5ml sp	2 tbsp	2 tbsp
Salt			
Cheese, grated	50g	2 oz	1 cup

Method
Place fish, lemon juice, a knob of butter and black pepper in a suitable container, cover and cook on HIGH for 2 minutes. Allow to cool before removing fish from the juice. Flake the fish, discarding bones and skin. Separately, make up the fish juices to 150ml/¼ pt/⅔ cup with the extra milk.

In a jug or suitable container, mix together the other 300ml/½ pt/1¼ cups milk with bay leaf, peppercorns, cloves and onion. Microwave this mixture, uncovered, on HIGH for 5 minutes.

Cover and cool. Strain the milk, discarding peppercorns and cloves. Chop onion and arrange the flaked fish and onion (mixed together) on four scallop shells or small shallow dishes. Stir the cornflour into the strained milk and then add in the fish juice/milk mix made earlier. Season with salt. Microwave this sauce on HIGH for 5 minutes, stirring twice. Spoon sauce over fish and sprinkle cheese over the top.

To serve: brown under grill.
To freeze: in same shells or dishes. Cool completely and cover.
Defrost for 7 minutes then allow 5 minutes *defrosting*-standing time.
Reheat: on HIGH for 3 minutes then brown quickly under grill.

HADDOCK VERONIQUE

This dish has a delicate appearance and texture – deceptively mouth-watering.

Serves: 4   *Freezer life: will not keep frozen*

Cook: Fish 5 minutes, onion sauce 3 minutes + 3 minutes.
Cooking-standing time: Fish 5 minutes, complete sauce 3 minutes.
Defrost:
Defrosting- standing time: } Not suitable for freezing.
Reheat: 3–5 minutes.

	Met.	Imp.	Am.
Haddock fillets	575g	1¼ lb	1¼ lb
Lemon juice	15ml sp	1 tbsp	1 tbsp
Butter	25g	1 oz	2 tbsp
Onion, finely chopped	1 small	1 small	1 small
Carton unsweetened natural yoghurt	150g	5 oz	small
White wine	150ml	¼ pt	⅔ cup
Green grapes, halved and de-pipped	50g	2 oz	2 oz
Salt and pepper			

Method
DEFROST the fish if necessary. This will need two stages: 1)

Microwave on DEFROST for 3 minutes, then allow a *defrosting*-standing time of 5 minutes. 2) Follow this with 3 more minutes on DEFROST and 5 minutes more *defrosting*-standing time.

Place the haddock fillets in a suitable shallow container. Sprinkle with the lemon juice and dot with half the butter. Cover and cook on HIGH for 5 minutes. Allow a *cooking*-standing time of 5 minutes.

In a suitable container or jug microwave the rest of the butter and the onion, covered, on HIGH for 3 minutes. Stir in the remaining ingredients, cover and cook on HIGH for 3 minutes. Allow a *cooking*-standing time of 3 minutes then pour the sauce over the fish.

Serve: With sauté potatoes or potato croquettes.
To reheat: Cover the dish and microwave on HIGH for 3–5 minutes taking care not to over-cook the fish.

POACHED FISH WITH CUCUMBER

Any white fish may be used in this quick but unusual recipe.

Serves: 4   *Freezer life: Not suitable for freezing*

Cook: Fish 5–7 minutes, sauce from juices 4–5 minutes.
Cooking-standing time: 5 minutes.
Defrost: }
Defrosting-standing time: } Will not keep frozen.
Reheat: 3–5 minutes.

	Met.	*Imp.*	*Am.*
White fish fillets or			
cutlets	575g	1¼ lb	1¼ lb
Milk	4×15ml sp	4 tbsp	4 tbsp
Mace	pinch	pinch	pinch
Salt and pepper			
Butter	knob	knob	knob
Cucumber, diced small	½	½	½

Method
DEFROST the fish if necessary. Microwave on DEFROST for 3 minutes then allow a *defrosting*-standing time of 5 minutes. Follow

this with 3 more minutes on DEFROST and 5 minutes more *defrosting*-standing time.

Arrange the fish in a suitable shallow container. Mix together the milk, mace and seasoning and pour this over the fish. Dot with the butter. Cover and cook on HIGH for 5–7 minutes. Pour off the fish juices into another suitable container. Re-cover the fish and allow a *cooking*-standing time of 5 minutes. Meanwhile stir the diced cucumber into the fish juices, cover and cook on HIGH for 4–5 minutes. Adjust seasoning if necessary and pour the mixture over the fish before serving.

Serve: With a platter of vegetables.
To reheat: Cover and microwave on HIGH for 3–5 minutes, taking care not to over-cook the fish.

FISH IN CURRY SAUCE

This recipe is ideal for the less expensive not-so-white coley.

Serves: 4   *Freezer life: 1 month*

Cook: Onions 3 minutes, sauce 8 minutes, sauce and fish 2 minutes.
Cooking-standing time: 10 minutes.
Defrost: 16 minutes. *Defrosting*-standing time: 10 minutes.
Reheat: 3–5 minutes.

	Met.	*Imp.*	*Am.*
Butter	25g	1 oz	2 tbsp
Onions, finely chopped	225g	8 oz	½ lb
Cornflour or cornstarch	15ml sp	1 tbsp	1 tbsp
Curry paste	2–3 × 15ml sp	2–3 tbsp	2–3 tbsp
Can tomatoes, chopped, including juice	397g	14 oz	medium
Chicken stock	300ml	½ pt	1¼ cups
Lemon juice	2 × 15ml sp	2 tbsp	2 tbsp
Sugar	2 × 5ml sp	2 tsp	2 tsp
Salt and black pepper			
White fish such as coley or cod, cut into bite-size pieces	450g	1 lb	1 lb

Method
DEFROST fish if necessary (see previous recipe).

Place the butter and onions in a suitable container, cover and cook on HIGH for 3 minutes. Stir in the cornflour then add the remaining ingredients (except the fish). Cover and cook on HIGH for 8 minutes, stirring twice. Stir in the fish pieces then cook on HIGH for 2 minutes. Allow a *cooking*-standing time of 10 minutes before serving.

Serve: On a bed of hot rice.
To freeze: Pour into a rigid polythene or microwave-freezer container, cool completely and freeze. DEFROST for about 16 minutes and allow a 10 minute *defrosting*-standing time. Then reheat on HIGH for 3–5 minutes taking care not to over-cook the fish.

MACKEREL IN CIDER

The cider and apples give a subtle flavour to the mackerel.

Serves: 4   *Freezer life: Not suitable*

Cook: 12–16 minutes. *Cooking*-standing time: 5 minutes.
Defrost:
Defrosting-standing time: } Will not keep frozen.
Reheat: 3–5 minutes.

	Met.	Imp.	Am.
Mackerel, gutted and cleaned	4	4	4
Butter	75g	3 oz	6 tbsp
Eating apples, peeled and grated	2	2	2
Lemon juice and grated rind	1	1	1
Onion, grated	1 small	1 small	1 small
Cheese, such as Cheddar, grated	50g	2 oz	2 oz
Fresh breadcrumbs	50g	2 oz	2 oz
Salt and pepper			
Dry cider	300ml	½ pt	1¼ cups
Parsley, chopped, to garnish			

Method
DEFROST the fish if necessary (see recipe on page 61).

In a basin melt 1 tbsp of the butter on HIGH (30–45 seconds) and mix into this the apples, lemon juice and rind, onion, cheese and breadcrumbs. Season to taste and use the mixture to stuff the mackerel. Arrange the fish in a large shallow dish (see page 16) and pour the cider over. Dot the mackerel with the remaining butter, cover and cook on HIGH for 12–16 minutes, depending on their size. Allow a *cooking*-standing time of 5 minutes before serving. Garnish with chopped parsley.

Serve: With vegetables or green salad.
To reheat: Microwave, covered, on HIGH for 3–5 minutes, taking care not to over-cook the fish.

VEGETABLES

Cooking fresh and frozen vegetables in the microwave oven is easy. They retain maximum colour and flavour and are crisply tender.

Points for microwaving fresh vegetables
Even-cut vegetables encourage even cooking.

Use the minimum amount of water (30–45ml/2–3 tbsp per 450g/1 lb vegetables) so that the minimum flavour and nutritional value is lost.

Whole vegetables, such as potatoes, corn-on-the-cob, mushrooms and courgettes, need only the water clinging to them after washing. Pierce the skins of whole vegetables such as potatoes, courgettes and tomatoes to prevent them bursting.

Canned vegetables should be turned out into a suitable container and covered before microwaving.

Cover fresh and frozen vegetables during microwave cooking.

Salt vegetables after cooking to avoid drying out and toughening of their surfaces.

Allow a *cooking*-standing time before serving.

Cooking times for *fresh* vegetables differ with types. Your manufacturer's instruction/recipe book will list times to suit your model. Most vegetables require a *cooking*-standing time too.

Blanching Vegetables
Up to 450g/1 lb of vegetables may be successfully blanched in your microwave oven. Large quantities may be more speedily blanched by the conventional method. As well as being advantageous for small amounts of vegetables, microwave blanching improves retention of those vitamins normally lost into the blanching water. It is also a convenient and clean process – minus a steamy kitchen. Vegetables can be blanched, cooled, frozen, defrosted and cooked in the same bag if wished. Check for the vegetable you are blanching, on the chart which follows. Always plan ahead and pack in suitable quantities for defrosting and cooking.

Method 1
1. Wash the vegetables thoroughly in cold water; trim or prepare normally according to their specific need. Sort into similar sizes and discard imperfect vegetables.
2. Place vegetables in a boil-in-bag. You do not need to add water. Tie loosely (so expanding air can escape) with string or cotton (not a plastic or paper-coated wire tie).
3. Blanch on HIGH for the recommended time, turning the bag over half way.
4. Plunge the bag immediately into ice cold water, ensuring no water enters the neck (I keep elastic bands handy to seal the opening when the bag comes out of the oven.) The bag must be

kept under the water until the vegetables are completely cool.
5. Dry the bag well, label and freeze.

Method 2
1. Wash the vegetables thoroughly in cold water, trim and prepare as usual according to type and sort into similar sizes. Discard any imperfect vegetables.
2. Place the vegetables in a suitable container, adding 45ml/3 tbsp water. Cover with lid or cling film (piercing to allow for the escape of steam).
3. Blanch on HIGH for the recommended time, stirring half way.
4. Drain the vegetables and plunge immediately into ice cold water until cool.
5. Drain the vegetables well.
6. Either: open freeze on trays before packing into freezer bags, boil-in-bags, or rigid containers,
   or: pack in suitable quantities for defrosting/cooking into freezer bags, boil-in-bags or rigid containers.

Vegetable blanching chart

Vegetable (450g/1 lb)	Size	Time on HIGH
Asparagus stalks	Large	3 minutes
	Medium	2½ minutes
	Small	2 minutes
Aubergine slices	1½cm/½ in	2 minutes
Beans, green/runner	Whole	2½ minutes
	Cut	2 minutes
	Sliced	1½ minutes
Beans, broad		2 minutes
Broccoli stalks	Large	3½ minutes
	Medium	2½ minutes
	Small	2 minutes
Brussels sprouts	Large	4 minutes
	Medium	3 minutes
	Small	2½ minutes

Vegetable (450g / 1 lb)	Size	Time on HIGH
Cabbage, shredded		2 minutes
Artichokes, globe	Whole	4 minutes
	Hearts	3 minutes
Jerusalem	Slices	2½ minutes
Carrot slices/sticks		3 minutes
Cauliflower florets		2½ minutes
Celery, sticks	5cm/2 in	3 minutes
hearts	Small	4 minutes
Corn-on-the-cob	Large	5 minutes
	Medium	4 minutes
	Small	3 minutes
Courgette slices	1½cm/½ in	1½ minutes
Leeks slices	2½cm/1 in	2 minutes

Mushrooms should be sautéed in a little butter for 1 minute, cooled, then frozen.

Onions, whole	Small	3 minutes
Parsnip slices	1½cm/½ in	3 minutes
Pepper/capsicum slices	½cm/¼ in	2 minutes
Turnip	Slices or small whole	3 minutes
Peas	Medium	2 minutes
	Small	1½ minutes
Spinach		1½ minutes
Swede dice	1½ cm/½ in	3 minutes
Sweetcorn		2½ minutes

FROZEN VEGETABLES

Cook frozen vegetables straight from the freezer. Simply place the vegetables in a suitable container, add water or butter (see table), cover and cook on HIGH for the recommended time. No intermediate *defrosting*-standing time (essential for nearly all other food) is required. Remember, blanched vegetables are partially cooked already.

Vegetable	Weight/quantity	Time on HIGH	Cooking-standing time	Hints
Asparagus	450g/1 lb	15 minutes	5 minutes	Add 60ml/4 tbsp water. Separate during defrosting.
	225g/8 oz	6-8 minutes	3 minutes	Add 30ml/2 tbsp water. Separate during defrosting.
Beans, broad	450g/1 lb	14 minutes	5 minutes	Add 75ml/5 tbsp water. Stir or shake during defrosting.
	225g/8 oz	7-8 minutes	3 minutes	Add 30ml/2 tbsp water. Stir or shake during defrosting.
Beans, green/runner	450g/1 lb	12 minutes	5 minutes	Add 90ml/6 tbsp water. Stir, etc.
	225g/8 oz	6-8 minutes	3 minutes	Add 45ml/3 tbsp water. Stir, etc.
Broccoli	225g/8 oz	8-10 minutes	7 minutes	Add 60ml/4 tbsp water. Separate during defrosting.

Vegetable	Weight/quantity	Time on HIGH	Cooking-standing time	Hints
Brussels sprouts	450g/1 lb	12 minutes	5 minutes	Add 60ml/4 tbsp water. Stir, etc.
	225g/8 oz	6-8 minutes	3 minutes	Add 30ml/2 tbsp water. Stir, etc.
Cabbage	450g/1 lb	12 minutes	3 minutes	Add 60ml/4 tbsp water. Separate during defrosting.
	225g/8 oz	6-8 minutes	3 minutes	Add 30ml/2 tbsp water. Separate during defrosting.
Carrots, sliced or baby	450g/1 lb	13-15 minutes	5-7 minutes	Add 60ml/4 tbsp water. Stir, etc.
	225g/8 oz	6-7 minutes	3-5 minutes	Add 30ml/2 tbsp water. Stir, etc.
Cauliflower florets	450g/1 lb	12 minutes	7 minutes	Add 30ml/2 tbsp water. Separate during defrosting.
	225g/8 oz	6-8 minutes	3-5 minutes	Add 15ml/1 tbsp water. Separate during defrosting.
Courgettes	450g/1 lb	12 minutes	5 minutes	Add 30ml/2 tbsp water. Separate during defrosting.
	225g/8 oz	6-8 minutes	3 minutes	Add 15ml/1 tbsp water. Separate during defrosting.

Vegetable	Weight/quantity	Time on HIGH	Cooking-standing time	Hints
Corn-on-the-cob	One	3-4 minutes	2 minutes	Dot with butter and wrap in greaseproof paper.
	Two	6-7 minutes	2 minutes	Ditto
Leeks	450g / 1 lb	15 minutes	5 minutes	Add 30ml/2 tbsp water. Separate during defrosting.
	225g / 8 oz	7-8 minutes	3 minutes	Add 15ml/1 tbsp water. Separate during defrosting.
Mixed vegetables	450g / 1 lb	10 minutes	5 minutes	Add 30ml/2 tbsp water. Stir, etc.
	225g / 8 oz	6 minutes	3 minutes	Add 15ml/1 tbsp water. Stir, etc.
Mushrooms	225g / 8 oz	5-6 minutes	2 minutes	Add knob of butter. Stir, etc.
Onions, sliced	225g / 8 oz	6-7 minutes	3 minutes	Add 30ml/2 tbsp water. Stir, etc.
Parsnips, diced	450g / 1 lb	15 minutes	7 minutes	Add 90ml/6 tbsp water. Stir, etc.
	225g / 8 oz	7-9 minutes	5 minutes	Add 45ml/3 tbsp water. Stir, etc.

Vegetable	Weight/quantity	Time on HIGH	Cooking-standing time	Hints
Peas	450g/1 lb	10 minutes	5 minutes	Add knob of butter. Stir, etc.
	225g/8 oz	5-6 minutes	3 minutes	Add knob of butter. Stir, etc.
Peas/carrots mix	225g/8 oz	7-8 minutes	5 minutes	Add knob of butter. Stir, etc.
Spinach	450g/1 lb	10 minutes	5 minutes	Add knob of butter. Stir, etc.
	225g/8 oz	6-8 minutes	3 minutes	Add knob of butter. Stir, etc.
Swede/turnip, diced	225g/8 oz	6-7 minutes	3 minutes	Add knob of butter. Stir, etc.
Sweetcorn	450g/1 lb	12 minutes	5 minutes	Add 60ml/4 tbsp water. Stir, etc.
	225g/8 oz	4-6 minutes	3 minutes	Add 30ml/2 tbsp water. Stir, etc.

Oven Chips

Your microwave oven will cook oven chips direct from frozen. Generally they will not be as crisp as when cooked in the conventional oven but if you are cooking only a small amount it is more economical on fuel, and quicker and cleaner too.

Browning Dish Method

Preheat browning dish on HIGH for 7–8 minutes. Spread 225g/8 oz/½ lb frozen oven-chips evenly over the dish in one layer. Cook uncovered on HIGH for 6–7 minutes. Allow 2–3 minutes *cooking*-standing time before serving.

Plate Method

The chips will be pale compared with the result obtained using a browning dish. Place two layers of kitchen paper on a suitable plate or dish. Spread over 225g/8 oz/½ lb frozen chips on to the paper evenly in one layer. Cook uncovered on HIGH for 6–7 minutes, then allow 2–3 minutes *cooking*-standing time before serving.

Combination Method

Oven-chips can be microwave cooked and browned in cookers with combined microwave/conventional ovens. Check your instruction book for the correct method for your model.

SAVOURY ONION AND PARSNIP BAKE

This is delicious with cold roast meats, boiled bacon, and fish. It makes a substantial meal for two served simply with green salad.

Serves: 4   *Freezer life: 6 months*

Cook: Vegetables 8 minutes, topping 3½ minutes, plus browning. *Cooking*-standing time: Vegetables – while preparing topping; topping sauce, 1 min.
Defrost: 10 mins. *Defrosting*-standing time: 10 mins.
Reheat: 8 mins., plus browning.

	Met.	Imp.	Am.
Onions, finely sliced	225g	8 oz	½ lb
Parsnips, finely sliced	225g	8 oz	½ lb
Salt and pepper			
Parsley, chopped	15ml sp	1 tbsp	1 tbsp
Water or white wine	45ml	3 tbsp	3 tbsp

Topping:

Flour	25g	1 oz	¼ cup
Milk	300ml	½ pt	1¼ cups
Butter or margarine	15g	½ oz	1 tbsp
Salt and pepper			
Egg, size 3, beaten	1	1	1

Method

Arrange half the onions in the base of a suitable shallow container or dish. Arrange half the parsnips on top. Season with salt and pepper and sprinkle over half the parsley. Repeat with another layer of onions, parsnips, seasoning and parsley. Pour over the water or wine. Cover and cook on HIGH for 8 minutes. The *cooking*-standing time can take place whilst you prepare the topping.

Topping: In a suitable jug or bowl mix the flour with a little of the milk to form a smooth paste. Gradually stir in the rest of the milk, season with salt and pepper and float the butter on top. Cook uncovered on HIGH for 3½ minutes (stirring well after 2 minutes). Allow a *cooking*-standing time of one minute then quickly stir in the beaten egg. Spread the sauce on top of the vegetables.

To serve: Brown under a conventional grill.
To freeze: Cool and freeze in same container.
Defrost in same covered container on DEFROST for 10 minutes, allow 10 minutes *defrosting*-standing time, then reheat on HIGH for 8 minutes. Brown under the grill.

BRAISED CHINESE LEAVES

The bacon gives this recipe a full flavour. Good with chicken.

Serves: 4 as main course
Serves: 6 as accompanying vegetable   *Freezer life: 6 weeks*

Cook: 2 mins + 12 mins. *Cooking*-standing time: 5 mins.
Defrost: 10–12 mins. *Defrosting*-standing time: 5 mins.
Reheat: 10 mins.

	Met.	Imp.	Am.
Butter	50g	2 oz	4 tbsp

Braised Chinese Leaves—contd.

Streaky bacon, chopped	100g	4 oz	¼ lb
Onion, finely chopped	1 small	1 small	1 small
Chinese leaves	1 head	1 head	1 head
Chicken stock, boiling	300ml	½ pt	1¼ cups
Salt and pepper			
Parsley, chopped	5ml sp	1 tsp	1 tsp
Thyme, fresh chopped	5ml sp	1 tsp	1 tsp
or dried	2.5ml sp	½ tsp	½ tsp

Method
Place butter, bacon and onion in a suitable large container or casserole, cover, cook on HIGH for 2 minutes (stir after 1 minute). Discard any outer blemished Chinese leaves and trim the base carefully. Cut into rounds about 6cm/1½ in thick. Arrange rounds on top of bacon mixture and pour the boiling stock over it (water from kettle or heated in microwave on HIGH for 3-4 minutes). Sprinkle with seasoning, parsley and thyme. Cover and cook on HIGH for 12 minutes, spooning the liquid over the Chinese leaves again once or twice during cooking.

To serve: Allow to rest for 5 minutes *cooking*-standing time.
To freeze: Cool completely and freeze in same container.
Defrost in same container (covered) for 10-12 minutes on DEFROST. Allow 5 minutes *defrosting*-standing time. Reheat on HIGH for 10 minutes.

LEEK PARCELS IN CHEESY SAUCE

This is a meal in itself with the leeks remaining beautifully whole.

Serves: 4   *Freezer life: 6 months*

Cook: Leeks 8 minutes, sauce 2½ minutes, whole 1½ minutes, plus browning. *Cooking*-standing time: Leeks 5 minutes; whole dish 5 minutes under grill.
Defrost: 8 minutes. *Defrosting*-standing time: 5 minutes.
Reheat: 5-8 minutes.

	Met.	Imp.	Am.
Butter or margarine	50g	2 oz	4 tbsp
Leeks	4	4	4
Black pepper, ground			
Plain flour	25g	1 oz	¼ cup
Milk	300ml	½ pt	1¼ cups
Salt			
Allspice (optional)	pinch	pinch	pinch
Egg, size 3, beaten	1	1	1
Ham slices, cooked			
pre-packed	4	4	4
Cheese, grated	50g	2 oz	¾ cup

Method
Place butter in a suitable container or casserole and melt on HIGH for 1 minute. Trim the leeks to about 15cm/6 in long and wash thoroughly (slit the dark green part down its length if necessary). Arrange leeks in the container (allow space between them) and brush the melted butter over them. Sprinkle with black pepper. Cover and cook on HIGH for 8 minutes (brushing the butter over the leeks again after 5 minutes).

Remove leeks from the butter, cover and leave aside for the *cooking*-standing time of 5 minutes. Stir flour into the butter then gradually add the milk, stirring well. Season with salt and allspice (optional). Cook on HIGH for 2½ minutes (stir after 1 minute) or until the sauce boils. Stir well and add the beaten egg. Wrap each leek in a slice of ham and arrange them in the container, spooning the sauce over. Cook on HIGH for 1½ minutes.

To serve: Sprinkle grated cheese over the top and brown under a conventional grill.
To freeze: Omit cheese, cool completely and freeze in same container.
Defrost in same covered container for 8 minutes on DEFROST then allow 5 minutes *defrosting*-standing time. Reheat on HIGH for 5-8 minutes. Sprinkle with cheese and brown under the grill.

CHANTILLY PEAS

Frozen peas take on a new lease of life in this recipe.

Serves: 4   *Freezer life: Not suitable*

Cook: Butter 1 minute, vegetables 4–5 minutes, complete 1 minute.
Cooking-standing time: 5 minutes.
Defrost:
Defrosting-standing time: } Will not keep frozen.
Reheat: 2–4 minutes.

	Met.	*Imp.*	*Am.*
Butter	**25g**	**1 oz**	**2 tbsp**
Frozen peas	**225g**	**8 oz**	**½ lb**
Frozen carrots	**100g**	**4 oz**	**¼ lb**
Lemon juice	**15ml sp**	**1 tbsp**	**1 tbsp**
Double or thick cream	**3 × 15ml sp**	**3 tbsp**	**3 tbsp**
Mint, chopped (optional)	**½ × 5ml sp**	**½ tsp**	**½ tsp**
Salt and black pepper			

Method
Place the butter in a suitable container and melt on HIGH for
45–60 seconds. Stir in the peas and carrots, cover and cook on
HIGH for 4–5 minutes. Allow a *cooking*-standing time of 5 minutes
then stir in the remaining ingredients. Cook on HIGH for 1 minute.
Allow a *cooking*-standing time of 5 minutes.

Serve as an accompaniment to meat or fish. It is delicious with a
sliced bacon joint.

To reheat cover and cook on HIGH for 2–4 minutes.

SAUCES

Sauces can be made in the serving jug or dish. Make them in advance and simply reheat them when ready to serve. Sauces do not stick and burn on the sides of the container as they do in saucepans so washing up is easy. Use a jug or container large enough to allow some bubbling up of the sauce (particularly those containing milk) and stir at least once or twice during cooking to prevent lumps forming. Instant sauces are made even more quickly and conveniently in a microwave oven. Cook a large amount of sauce at one time – it takes only marginally longer. Then cool completely and freeze in suitable amounts for defrosting and reheating at a later date.

BASIC WHITE SAUCE

The consistency of this sauce is suitable for pouring over fish, vegetables or bacon. Flavour variations are given below.

Serves: 4–6   *Freeze life: 6 months*

Cook: Butter 1 minute, sauce 5–6 minutes. *Cooking*-standing time: 3 minutes.
Defrost: 10–12 minutes. *Defrosting*-standing time: 10 minutes.
Reheat: 3–4 minutes.

Basic White Sauce—contd.

	Met.	Imp.	Am.
Butter	25g	1 oz	2 tbsp
Flour	25g	1 oz	3 tbsp
Salt and pepper			
Milk	500ml	1 pt	2½ cups

Method
Place the butter in a suitable container or jug. Melt on HIGH for 1 minute. Add the flour and seasoning and gradually stir in the milk. Cook uncovered on HIGH for 5–6 minutes, stirring at least twice, or until the sauce boils. Allow a *cooking*-standing time of 3 minutes.

To freeze: Pour into a rigid polythene container or microwave-freezer container and cool completely before freezing.
Defrost covered for 10–12 minutes, breaking up the sauce with a fork. Allow a *defrosting*-standing time of 10 minutes before reheating on HIGH for 3–4 minutes.
Variations: Flavour the sauce with grated cheese, lightly-cooked mushrooms (or onions), chopped parsley (or capers), chopped fresh herbs, or chopped hard-boiled eggs.

SPICY TOMATO SAUCE

A sauce with a bite to serve with beefburgers, meatballs, white fish or vegetables.

Serves: 4   *Freezer life: 1 year*

Cook: Onion 3 minutes, sauce 7 minutes. *Cooking*-standing time: 5 minutes.
Defrost: 10–12 minutes. *Defrosting*-standing time: 10 minutes.
Reheat: 3–4 minutes.

	Met.	Imp.	Am.
Butter	25g	1 oz	2 tbsp
Onion, chopped finely	1 small	1 small	1 small
Flour	15ml sp	1 tbsp	1 tbsp
Tin tomatoes, chopped, including juice	397g	14 oz	medium

Dried oregano	½ × 5ml sp	½ tsp	½ tsp
Dried basil	½ × 5ml sp	½ tsp	½ tsp
Tomato purée or paste	2 × 15ml sp	2 tbsp	2 tbsp
Tabasco sauce	2 drops	2 drops	2 drops
Salt and black pepper			

Method
Place the butter and onion in a suitable container or jug. Cover and cook on HIGH for 3 minutes. Stir in the flour then add the remaining ingredients. Cover and cook on HIGH for a further 7 minutes. Allow a *cooking*-standing time of 5 minutes before serving.

To freeze: Cool completely and pour into a rigid polythene or microwave-freezer container.
Defrost for 10–12 minutes, breaking the sauce up with a fork. Allow a 10 minute *defrosting*-standing time before reheating on HIGH for 3–4 minutes.

SWEET'N'SOUR SAUCE

This sauce is a favourite served with sausages.

Serves: 4 *Freezer life: 3 months*

Cook: 3–4 minutes. *Cooking*-standing time: 5 minutes.
Defrost: 6–8 minutes. *Defrosting*-standing time: 5 minutes.
Reheat: 2 minutes.

	Met.	*Imp.*	*Am.*
Cornflour or cornstarch	15ml sp	1 tbsp	1 tbsp
Water	150ml	¼ pt	⅔ cup
Soy sauce	3 × 15ml sp	3 tbsp	3 tbsp
Tomato ketchup	4 × 15ml sp	4 tbsp	4 tbsp
White wine vinegar	2 × 15ml sp	2 tbsp	2 tbsp
Sugar	15ml sp	1 tbsp	1 tbsp
Salt and pepper			

Method
In a suitable container or jug mix the cornflour with a little of the water. Stir in the remaining water and the rest of the ingredients. Cover and cook on HIGH for 3–4 minutes, stirring occasionally, or

until the sauce boils. Allow a 5 minute *cooking*-standing time before serving.

To freeze: Cool completely and pour into a rigid polythene or microwave-freezer container.
Defrost for 6–8 minutes, breaking sauce up with a fork. Allow a 5 minute *defrosting*-standing time before reheating for about 2 minutes.

NUTTY BUTTERSCOTCH SAUCE

Serve this hot with ice cream or cooked whole fruit such as baked apples.

Serves: 4–6　　　　　　　　　　　　　*Freezer life: 4 months*

Cook: 5 minutes. *Cooking*-standing time: 5 minutes.
Defrost: 6–8 minutes. *Defrosting*-standing time: 10 minutes.
Reheat: 2–3 minutes.

	Met.	Imp.	Am.
Cornflour or cornstarch	2 × 15ml sp	2 tbsp	2 tbsp
Milk	300ml	½ pt	1¼ cups
Brown sugar	100g	4 oz	1 cup
Golden syrup	2 × 15ml sp	2 tbsp	2 tbsp
Vanilla essence	few drops	few drops	few drops
Butter	40g	1½ oz	3 tbsp
Hazelnuts or walnuts, chopped	25g	1 oz	1 oz

Method
In a suitable container or jug mix the cornflour with a little of the milk. Stir in the remaining ingredients (except the nuts). Cook, uncovered, on HIGH for about 5 minutes, stirring two or three times, or until the sauce boils. Allow a *cooking*-standing time of 5 minutes before stirring in the nuts.

Serve: See above.
To freeze: Cool completely in a rigid polythene container or microwave-freezer container.
Defrost for 6–8 minutes and allow a *defrosting*-standing time of 10 minutes. Reheat on HIGH for 2–3 minutes.

FRUITY SAUCE

Serve this sauce hot or cold with sponge or suet puddings. It is
equally delicious poured over ice cream and cold sweets.

Serves: 4–6   *Freezer life: 6 months*

Cook: 10 minutes + 1 minute. *Cooking*-standing time: Nil.
Defrost: 6–8 minutes. *Defrosting*-standing time: 10 minutes.
Reheat: 2–3 minutes.

	Met.	Imp.	Am.
Frozen raw fruit such as raspberries, blackberries, red or blackcurrants, gooseberries, strawberries	450g	1 lb	1 lb
Water	4×15ml sp	4 tbsp	4 tbsp
Caster sugar	125g	4 oz	½ cup

Method
Place the frozen fruit and the water in a suitable container, cover
and cook on HIGH for 10 minutes, stirring occasionally. Stir in the
sugar and cook on HIGH for a further 1 minute. Blend the sauce or
press it through a fine sieve.

To serve: See above.
To freeze: Cool completely, pour into a rigid polythene container
or microwave-freezer container and freeze.
Defrost for 6–8 minutes and allow a 10 minute *defrosting*-standing
time. Reheat on HIGH for 2–3 minutes.

ORANGE CHOCOLATE SAUCE

A light sauce to serve with chocolate pudding, ice cream or whole
bananas baked for 3 minutes in the microwave.

Serves: 4   *Freezer life: 1 month*

Cook: 2 minutes. *Cooking*-standing time: Nil.

Defrost: 1–2 minutes. *Defrosting*-standing time: 5 minutes.
Reheat: 1–2 minutes.

	Met.	Imp.	Am.
Plain chocolate, broken into squares	100g	4 oz	1/4 lb
Golden syrup	3 × 15ml sp	3 tbsp	3 tbsp
Butter	40g	1 1/2 oz	3 tbsp
Orange, grated rind and juice	1	1	1

Method
Place all the ingredients in a suitable container, cover and cook on HIGH for 2 minutes. Beat the sauce well to a smooth consistency. If it cools and thickens reheat on HIGH for a minute or two.

To freeze: Pour into a rigid polythene container or microwave-freezer container and cool completely before freezing.
Before serving defrost for 1–2 minutes and allow a 5 minute *defrosting*-standing time. Then reheat on HIGH for 1–2 minutes before serving.

MEAT

Meat cooked in the microwave oven is full of flavour and natural juices. Microwaving is a particularly clean method of cooking meat too – with less oven cleaning. As with conventional methods the quality of meat will dictate the finished result.

Points for microwaving meat
Best results are achieved if the meat (particularly a joint) is cooked from room temperature.

Frozen meat should be completely defrosted before cooking, allowing the appropriate *defrosting*-standing time (see chart on page 37). Defrost joints covered, turning once during defrosting. Solid blocks of meat, such as mince, should be broken up with a fork during defrosting. Roast meat on a suitable roasting rack (or upturned saucer) in a large dish (to catch the juices – the meat should not sit in its own juices). Cover the joint with a slit roasting bag.

Salt meat *after* microwaving (except the skin of roast pork) to avoid drying out and toughening the meat fibres.

Large joints will brown naturally in the microwave oven since their cooking times are longer than smaller items such as chops and steaks. The latter may be browned (by frying or grilling) before or after microwave cooking. Brushing with unsalted butter helps meat to brown, as does covering with a lid, or roast-a-bag (remember to pierce bags to allow steam to escape).

Choose even-shaped pieces of meat to encourage even cooking. Prevent overcooking of thinner parts of joints by covering small areas with foil – check with your instruction book for specific instructions. When arranging chops on a plate or dish, place the thicker ends to the outer edge.

Mince mixtures can be shaped into balls, small loaves or into a ring mould for speedier, more even cooking. When cooking mince (e.g. for bolognese sauce) break up the meat with a fork during cooking.

Cover meat and meat dishes during cooking to prevent splashing the oven walls with spitting fat.

Wooden skewers should be used to secure meat.

Less liquid will be required for casseroles since less evaporation takes place during microwave cooking. Even-cut pieces of meat and vegetables will encourage even cooking. It is best to brown the meat (mince and pieces) in the microwave oven and drain off the fat (if wished) before adding the remaining ingredients.

Casseroles are best cooked on a LOW setting to imitate the long, slow cooking of conventional casseroling. Your instruction book will give you guidance on this. If your oven does not have such variable control the meat will be more tender and flavoursome if the casserole is microwaved and allowed to cool and then reheated. During the cooking and reheating periods food flavours have time to develop and intermingle.

The following table may be used as a guide to cooking meat. Allow a 15–20 minute *cooking*-standing time.

		Minutes per 450g/1 lb on HIGH
Beef (a boneless joint cooks more quickly than one with a bone)	Rare	5–7
	Medium	6½–8½
	Well done	7–10
Lamb		8–10
Pork		9–11
Veal		9–10

Meat thermometers
These are used to test birds and meat joints for 'doneness'. Use only specially-designed non-metal meat thermometers during microwave cooking. After cooking, the bird or joint should be allowed a *cooking*-standing time (see chart on page 98). Cover it with foil with the meat thermometer inserted in the thickest part (*not* against the bone for joints: see Fig. 2 for poultry). The internal temperature should rise by 5–7°C (10–15°F) during this time.

Meat thermometer temperatures:

	°C	°F
Beef rare	60	140
medium	71	160
well done	79	174
Lamb medium	77	170
well done	82	180
Pork should always be well done	88	190

When the meat has reached the appropriate temperature it is cooked.
See also 'Microwave Thermometers' on page 30.

GINGERY MINCE WITH DUMPLINGS

This is a particularly easy, economical family meal.

Serves: 4   *Freezer life: 2 months*

Cook: Meat 5 minutes + 15 minutes, meat and dumplings 6 minutes. *Cooking*-standing time: 5 minutes.
Defrost: 10 minutes. *Defrosting*-standing time: 5 minutes.
Reheat: Meat 4 minutes, meat and dumplings 6 minutes.

	Met.	*Imp.*	*Am.*
Minced beef	600g	1¼ lb	1 ¼ lb
Onions, finely chopped	225g	8 oz	½ lb
Mushrooms, chopped	100g	4 oz	¼ lb
Can tomatoes, roughly chopped	397g	14 oz	medium
Ginger, ground	3 × 2.5ml sp	1½ tsp	1½ tsp
Salt and pepper			
Paprika	5ml sp	1 tsp	1 tsp
Parsley, chopped	15ml sp	1 tbsp	1 tbsp

Dumplings:

Self-raising flour	100g	4 oz	1 cup
Baking powder	2.5ml sp	½ tsp	½ tsp
Salt	pinch	pinch	pinch
Beef suet, shredded	50g	2 oz	½ cup
Water			

Method
Defrost minced beef if necessary, breaking it up with a fork as it thaws. Allow 5–10 minutes *defrosting*-standing time.

Place minced beef in a suitable deep container or casserole. Cook on HIGH for 5 minutes and stir well with a fork to separate all the pieces. Then stir in the onions, mushrooms, tomatoes, ginger, salt and pepper and paprika. Cook on HIGH for 15 minutes (stir after 8 minutes). Stir in the parsley and adjust seasoning if necessary.
Dumplings: Sift flour, baking powder and salt into a basin. Stir in suet. Mix to a soft dough with water. Shape into eight balls and arrange on top of the mince. Cover and cook on HIGH for 6 minutes. Allow a *cooking*-standing time (covered) of 5 minutes before serving.

To freeze: Omit dumplings, cool completely and freeze in same container or microwave-freezer container.
Defrost 10 minutes, breaking it up with fork as it thaws. Allow 5

minutes *defrosting*-standing time.
Reheat (covered) on HIGH for 4 minutes, add dumplings and continue as above, cooking on HIGH for 6 minutes and allowing a 5 minute *cooking*-standing time.

CASSEROLED BACON AND BUTTER BEANS

This is a creamy casserole. No salt is needed since plenty is given out of the bacon.

Serves: 4   *Freezer life: 6 weeks*

Cook: Onion 2 minutes + bacon 10 minutes + soup 10 minutes.
Cooking-standing time: 10 minutes.
Defrost: 10 minutes. *Defrosting*-standing time: 10 minutes.
Reheat: 5 minutes.

	Met.	Imp.	Am.
Smoked bacon, collar or gammon, cut into 2cm/ 1 in cubes	900g	2 lb	2 lb
Onion, chopped	225g	8 oz	½ lb
Butter	15ml sp	1 tbsp	1 tbsp
Black pepper, ground			
Can cream of mushroom soup	425g	15oz	medium
Can butter beans, drained	425g	15 oz	medium

Method
Place bacon cubes in a saucepan, cover with cold water and bring to the boil slowly on the conventional hob. Meanwhile place the onion and butter in a suitable large casserole or container, cover and cook on HIGH for 2 minutes.

Drain the bacon cubes well and stir into the onions. Season with black pepper. Cover and cook on HIGH for 10 minutes. Stir in the soup and continue cooking on HIGH for 10 minutes. Allow to stand, covered, for 10 minutes *cooking*-standing time.

To serve: With fried or roast potatoes and green vegetables or carrots.

To freeze: Cool completely and freeze in same container.
Defrost in same covered container on DEFROST for 10 minutes.
Allow a 10 minute *defrosting*-standing time and then reheat on
HIGH for 5 minutes.

PORK AND MUSHROOM CREAM

This dish is perfect for a special occasion.

Serves: 4   *Freezer life: 6 weeks*

Cook: Onion 3 minutes, pork 15 minutes + 8 minutes, with cream 1
minute. *Cooking*-standing time: 15 minutes.
Defrost: 8–10 minutes. *Defrosting*-standing time: 10 minutes.
Reheat: 7–10 minutes.

	Met.	Imp.	Am.
Pork fillet, cut into thin strips	700g	1½ lb	1½ lb
Butter	50g	2 oz	4 tbsp
Onion, sliced thinly	225g	8 oz	½ lb
Salt and black pepper			
Mace	pinch	pinch	pinch
Button mushrooms	350g	12 oz	¾ lb
Dry sherry	100ml	4 fl oz	½ cup
Carton double or thick cream	170ml	6 fl oz	small

Method
Defrost the pork if necessary for 5–6 minutes. Allow a 10 minute
defrosting-standing time.

Place the butter and onion into a suitable container. Cover and
cook on HIGH for 3 minutes. Stir in the pork strips, cover and cook
on HIGH for 15 minutes, stirring occasionally to separate the meat.
Season with salt and pepper then stir in the mace, button
mushrooms and dry sherry. Cover and cook again on HIGH for 8
minutes. Allow a *cooking*-standing time of 15 minutes. Stir in the
cream and reheat on HIGH for 1 minute (but do not boil).

To serve: Good with rice and green salad.
To freeze: Omit cream, cool completely and freeze in same
container or pour into a microwave-freezer container.

Defrost for 8–10 minutes on DEFROST. Allow a 10 minute *defrosting*-standing time.
Reheat covered on HIGH for 7–10 minutes, stir in the cream and heat on HIGH for one more minute (but do not allow it to boil).

BACON AND APPLE PUDDING

This is a light pudding cooked in minutes – and no steamy kitchen. Use leftovers from a cooked bacon joint.

Serves: 4   *Freezer life: 1 month*

Cook: 12 minutes. *Cooking*-standing time: 10 minutes.
Defrost: 6 minutes. *Defrosting*-standing time: 10 minutes.
Reheat: 5–7 minutes.

	Met.	Imp.	Am.
Pastry:			
Self-raising flour	225g	8 oz	2 cups
Salt	pinch	pinch	pinch
Suet, shredded	100g	4 oz	¼ lb
Water to mix			
Filling:			
Bacon, cooked and chopped finely	225g	8 oz	½ lb
Onion, chopped finely	1	1	1
Mushrooms, chopped finely	50g	2 oz	2 oz
Sharp eating apple, peeled, cored and roughly grated	1	1	1
Dried sage	5ml sp	1 tsp	1 tsp
Chicken stock	150ml	¼ pint	⅔ cup
Black pepper			

Method
Pastry: Sift flour and salt into a bowl and mix in the suet. Add sufficient water to make a soft dough, stirring well with a knife. Roll out two-thirds of the dough and use it to line a 900ml/1½ pint basin. Roll the remaining third into a circle large enough to form a lid.
Filling: Mix together all the ingredients and pour this into the

pastry-lined bowl. Place the lid on top and pinch the edges together to seal it securely. Cover and cook on HIGH for 12 minutes. Allow a 10 minute *cooking*-standing time.

To serve: With vegetables and a sauce such as Spicy Tomato Sauce on page 78.
To freeze: Cool completely and freeze in same container.
Defrost for about 6 minutes on DEFROST, allowing a 10 minute *defrosting*-standing time.
Reheat, covered, on HIGH for 5–7 minutes.

SAVOURY LIVER AND BACON

The Worcestershire sauce adds 'spice' to this dish.

Serves: 4   *Freezer life: 6 weeks*

Cook: Onion/bacon 3 minutes, liver 10 minutes. *Cooking*-standing time 10 minutes.
Defrost: 6–8 minutes. *Defrosting*-standing time: 10 minutes.
Reheat: 10 minutes.

	Met.	*Imp.*	*Am.*
Lamb's liver, sliced thinly	**450g**	**1 lb**	**1 lb**
Butter	**25g**	**1 oz**	**2 tbsp**
Onion, chopped	**1**	**1**	**1**
Streaky bacon, de-rinded and chopped	**4 rashers**	**4 rashers**	**4 rashers**
Beef stock or bouillon	**150ml**	**¼ pint**	**⅔ cup**
Tomato purée	**2×15ml sp**	**2 tbsp**	**2 tbsp**
Worcestershire sauce	**15ml sp**	**1 tbsp**	**1 tbsp**
Salt and black pepper			
Parsley, chopped, to garnish			

Method
Defrost the liver if necessary, on DEFROST, for 8–10 minutes, allowing a 5 minute *defrosting*-standing time.
  Place the butter, onion and bacon into a suitable container, cover and cook on HIGH for 3 minutes. Stir in the liver. Mix together the beef stock, tomato purée, Worcestershire sauce and seasoning, and pour this over the liver mixture. Cover and cook on HIGH for 10

minutes, stirring once or twice. Allow a *cooking*-standing time of 10 minutes.

To serve: With rice, noodles or croûtons, garnished with chopped parsley.
To freeze: Omit parsley, cool completely and freeze in same or a microwave-freezer container.
Defrost for 6–8 minutes on DEFROST, allowing a *defrosting*-standing time of 10 minutes.
Reheat, covered, on HIGH for 10 minutes.

BOEUF BOURGIGNON

A deliciously rich casserole.

Serves: 4   *Freezer life: 6 weeks*

Cook: Bacon 3 minutes, complete 20 minutes. *Cooking*-standing time: 15 minutes.
Defrost: 8–10 minutes. *Defrosting*-standing time: 15 minutes.
Reheat: 12 minutes.

	Met.	Imp.	Am.
Sirloin steak, cubed	700g	1½ lb	1½ lb
Streaky bacon, de-rinded and chopped	100g	4 oz	¼ lb
Cornflour or cornstarch	15ml sp	1 tbsp	1 tbsp
Baby onions, whole	100g	4 oz	¼ lb
Button mushrooms	175g	6 oz	6 oz
Garlic clove, crushed	2	2	2
Bouquet garni	1	1	1
Salt and black pepper			
Red wine	150ml	¼ pint	⅔ cup

Method
Defrost steak if necessary for 10–12 minutes on DEFROST, allowing a 10 minute *defrosting*-standing time.
    Place the bacon in a suitable large container, cover, and cook on HIGH for 3 minutes. Add the cornflour and stir well. Mix in the remaining ingredients. Cover and cook on HIGH for about 20 minutes or until the meat is cooked. Allow a *cooking*-standing time of 15 minutes before serving.

To serve: Remove bouquet garni and serve with rice or buttered noodles.

To freeze: Cool completely and freeze in same or a microwave-
freezer container.
Defrost for 8–10 minutes on DEFROST and allow a 15 minute
defrosting-standing time.
Reheat on HIGH for 12 minutes.

SAVOURY MEATBALLS IN TOMATOES

An economical and filling meal any time of the year.

Serves: 4   *Freezer life: 3 months*

Cook: Meatballs 6 minutes, complete 10 minutes. *Cooking*-
standing time: 10 minutes.
Defrost: 8–10 minutes. *Defrosting*-standing time: 15 minutes.
Reheat: 10 minutes.

	Met.	Imp.	Am.
Minced beef	450g	1 lb	1 lb
Breadcrumbs, fresh	25g	1 oz	1 oz
Onion, chopped finely or grated	small	small	small
Celery stick, chopped finely	1	1	1
Oregano, dried	5ml sp	1 tsp	1 tsp
Parmesan cheese, grated	2×15ml sp	2 tbsp	2 tbsp
Salt and black pepper			
Egg, size 3, beaten	1	1	1
Can tomatoes, including juice	397g	14 oz	medium
Parsley, chopped, to garnish			

Method
Defrost the beef if necessary for 8–10 minutes on DEFROST,
allowing a 10 minute *defrosting*-standing time.
　Mix together all the ingredients except the tomatoes and parsley.
Shape the mixture into 20 meatballs and arrange them in a large
suitable container. Cover and cook on HIGH for 6 minutes,
turning the meatballs over half way. Season the tomatoes
(including their juice) with salt and black pepper and pour this over
the meatballs. Cover and cook on HIGH for about 10 minutes,
stirring once or twice. Allow a 10 minute *cooking*-standing time.

To serve: Garnished with chopped parsley. Good with buttered spaghetti or jacket potatoes and green salad.
To freeze: Cool completely and freeze in same or a microwave-freezer container.
Defrost for 8–10 minutes on DEFROST, allowing a *defrosting*-standing time of 15 minutes.
Reheat on HIGH for about 10 minutes.

LAMB GOULASH

A deliciously unusual way of preparing lamb.

Serves: 4   *Freezer life: 2 months*

Cook: Lamb/onion 5 minutes, complete 25 minutes. *Cooking*-standing time: 10 minutes.
Defrost: 8–10 minutes. *Defrosting*-standing time: 15 minutes.
Reheat: 12 minutes.

	Met.	*Imp.*	*Am.*
Lamb, lean, cut into cubes	700g	1½ lb	1½ lb
Cooking oil	2 × 15ml sp	2 tbsp	2 tbsp
Onion, chopped	1	1	1
Flour	2 × 15ml sp	2 tbsp	2 tbsp
Can tomatoes, including			
juice	397g	14 oz	medium
Bay leaves	2	2	2
Red wine or stock	150ml	¼ pint	⅔ cup
Paprika pepper	2 × 5 ml sp	2 tsp	2 tsp
Salt and pepper			
Carton natural yoghurt	4 × 15ml sp	4 tbsp	4 tbsp
Green pepper, chopped	15ml sp	1 tbsp	1 tbsp

Method
Defrost the lamb if necessary on DEFROST for 10 minutes and allow a 15 minute *defrosting*-standing time.
   Place the lamb, cooking oil and onion into a suitable large container, cover and cook on HIGH for 5 minutes, stirring once or twice. Stir in the flour and mix well. Add the remaining ingredients (except yoghurt and green pepper), stirring well, cover and cook on HIGH for 25 minutes, stirring once or twice during cooking. Stir in the yoghurt and allow a 10 minute *cooking*-standing time.

To serve: Remove the bay leaves and sprinkle the chopped green pepper over. Serve with creamed potatoes.

To freeze: Omit yoghurt, cool completely and freeze in a microwave-freezer container.

Defrost for 8–10 minutes on DEFROST, allowing a 15 minute *defrosting*-standing time.

Reheat on HIGH for 12 minutes.

MIXED MEATS LOAF

Serve hot or cold any time of the year. Useful for picnics, parties and packed lunches.

Serves: 6   *Freezer life: 6 weeks*

Cook: Bacon/onion 5 minutes, meats 5 minutes, complete 20 minutes.

Cooking-standing time: 10 minutes.

Defrost: 10 minutes + 5 minutes. *Defrosting*-standing time: 5 minutes + 10 minutes.

Reheat: 6–7 minutes.

	Met.	*Imp.*	*Am.*
Streaky bacon, de-rinded and chopped finely	100g	4 oz	¼ lb
Onion, large, chopped finely or grated	1	1	1
Minced beef	450g	1 lb	1 lb
Pork sausagemeat	100g	4 oz	¼ lb
Breadcrumbs, fresh	100g	4 oz	¼ lb
Tomato purée	2 × 15ml sp	2 tbsp	2 tbsp
Worcestershire sauce	few drops	few drops	few drops
Dried mixed herbs	5ml sp	1 tsp	1 tsp
Salt and black pepper			
Mushrooms, chopped	100g	4 oz	¼ lb
Chopped parsley	15ml sp	1 tbsp	1 tbsp
Decoration:			
Tomato, sliced	1	1	1
Green pepper rings			
Mushroom slices			

Method

Place the bacon and onion into a suitable container, cover and cook on HIGH for 5 minutes. Mix in the minced beef and sausagemeat and cook, covered, on HIGH for 5 minutes. Mix in the remaining ingredients well. Line a 17½cm/7 inch diameter (straight-sided) dish with greaseproof paper. Arrange the decoration pieces of tomato, pepper and mushroom slices in the base of the dish. Empty the meat mixture carefully on top of the decoration and press it level. Cover and cook on HIGH for 20 minutes. Allow a 10 minute *cooking*-standing time.

To serve: Hot with Spicy Tomato Sauce (page 78), and jacket potatoes or cold (allow to cool in the container) with salads.
To freeze: Cool completely, turn out of the container, wrap in foil.
Defrost for 10 minutes on DEFROST, allowing a 5 minute *defrosting*-standing time; then for a further 5 minutes, allowing another 10 minute *defrosting*-standing time.
Reheat if wished on HIGH for 6-7 minutes.

ESCALOPES OF VEAL WITH ORANGE

An impressive main course. The orange delicately flavours the veal.

Serves: 4   *Freezer life: 1 month*

Cook: Butter/mushroom 5 minutes + 2 minutes, veal 7 minutes, complete 2-3 minutes. *Cooking*-standing time: 10 minutes.
Defrost: 6-8 minutes. *Defrosting*-standing time: 10 minutes.
Reheat: 5-7 minutes.

	Met.	*Imp.*	*Am.*
Veal escalopes	4	4	4
Butter	50g	2 oz	4 tbsp
Garlic clove, crushed	1	1	1
Button mushrooms, sliced	225g	8 oz	½ lb
Salt and black pepper			
Cornflour or cornstarch	15ml sp	1 tbsp	1 tbsp
Juice of orange	1	1	1
Oranges, peeled and divided into segments (skinned)	2	2	2

Method
Defrost the veal escalopes if necessary on DEFROST for 6–7
minutes, allowing a 10 minute *defrosting*-standing time.

Place the butter, garlic, mushrooms, salt and pepper in a large
shallow suitable container, cover and cook on HIGH for 5 minutes.
Stir in the cornflour, and orange juice, cover and cook on HIGH
for 2 minutes. Add the veal escalopes and spoon the mushroom
mixture over. Cover and cook on HIGH for about 7 minutes.
Arrange the orange segments over the top, cover and cook again on
HIGH for 2–3 minutes. Allow a 10 minute *cooking*-standing time.

To serve: Good with sauté, croquette or duchesse potatoes.
To freeze: Omit orange segments, cool completely and freeze in
same or a microwave-freezer container.
Defrost for 6–8 minutes on DEFROST, allowing a 10 minute
defrosting-standing time.
Reheat on HIGH for 5–7 minutes.

LAMB CHOPS IN FRUITY SAUCE

A spiced fruity recipe.

Serves: 4   *Freezer life: 1 month*

Cook: Chops 10 minutes, sauce 3 minutes + 5 minutes. *Cooking*-
standing time: 10 minutes.
Defrost: 10 minutes. *Defrosting*-standing time: 10 minutes.
Reheat: 8–10 minutes.

	Met.	*Imp.*	*Am.*
Lamb chops	8 small	8 small	8 small
Butter	15g	½ oz	1 tbsp
Garlic, crushed	1 clove	1 clove	1 clove
Onion, chopped finely	1 small	1 small	1 small
Cornflour or cornstarch	5ml sp	1 tsp	1 tsp
Clear honey	15ml sp	1 tbsp	1 tbsp
Mustard, made	5ml sp	1 tsp	1 tsp
Ginger	½ × 5ml sp	½ tsp	½ tsp
Eating apple, peeled and chopped	1	1	1
Raisins	50g	2 oz	2 oz
Dry cider	150ml	¼ pint	⅔ cup
Salt and black pepper			

Method
Defrost the chops if necessary for 10 minutes on DEFROST, allowing a 15 minute *defrosting*-standing time.

Arrange the chops in a large shallow container, dot each with butter, cover and cook on HIGH for 10 minutes, turning over half way. Remove chops to a hot serving dish, cover with foil and allow a 10 minute *cooking*-standing time. Into the lamb juices stir the garlic and onion. Cover and cook on HIGH for 3 minutes. Mix in the cornflour and then the remaining ingredients. Cover and cook on HIGH for 5 minutes.

To serve: Pour the hot sauce over the chops and serve with plain vegetables or rice.
To freeze: Pour the sauce over the chops and cool completely. Freeze in a microwave-freezer container.
Defrost for 10 minutes on DEFROST, allowing a 10 minute *defrosting*-standing time.
Reheat on HIGH for 8–10 minutes.

PORK FRICASSÉE

Pork chunks in a creamy sauce.

Serves: 4   *Freezer life: 2 months*

Cook: Pork 10 minutes, butter 30 seconds, complete 15 minutes.
Cooking-standing time: 10 minutes.
Defrost: 10–12 minutes. *Defrosting*-standing time: 10 minutes.
Reheat: 8–10 minutes.

	Met.	Imp.	Am.
Lean pork (such as shoulder), cubed	700g	1½ lb	1½ lb
Onion, chopped	1	1	1
Dry cider	150ml	¼ pint	⅔ cup
Bay leaf	1	1	1
Dried sage	5ml sp	1 tsp	1 tsp
Salt and black pepper			
Milk			
Butter	25g	1 oz	2 tbsp
Flour	25g	1 oz	2 tbsp
Button mushrooms, sliced	100g	4 oz	¼ lb

Method
Defrost pork if necessary on DEFROST for 5–6 minutes, allowing
a 10 minute *defrosting*-standing time.

   Place pork cubes, onion, cider, bay leaf, sage and seasoning in a
suitable container, cover and cook on HIGH for 10 minutes. Lift
out the pork, using a draining spoon and set to one side. Make up
the pork juices to 300ml/ ½ pint with milk. Place the butter into a
bowl or jug, melt on HIGH for 30 seconds. Stir in the flour then
gradually stir in the pork liquid. Mix in the pork cubes and
mushrooms. Cover and cook on HIGH for 15 minutes, stirring
twice during cooking. Allow a 10 minute *cooking*-standing time.

To serve: On a bed of rice or with sauté potatoes.
To freeze: Cool completely and freeze in same or a microwave-
freezer container.
Defrost for 10–12 minutes on DEFROST, allowing a *defrosting*-
standing time of 10 minutes.
Reheat on HIGH for 8–10 minutes.

POULTRY

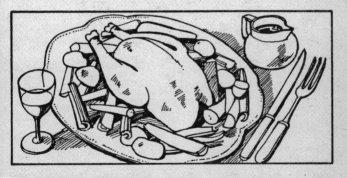

Microwave-cooked poultry is succulently moist and tender. All
poultry – whole birds, joints or pieces – adapt well to microwave
cooking.

Points for microwaving poultry

Cook whole birds on a suitable roasting rack in a large container (to catch the juices). The bird should not sit in the juices. Cover with a slit roasting bag to assist browning and avoid splattering the oven walls.

Choose even-sized pieces or joints for evenly cooked results. Arrange thicker areas towards the outer edge of the cooking container and thinner ends towards the centre (for example, drumsticks).

Browning is improved if the skin of a whole bird is brushed with unsalted butter, or diluted yeast extract. Alternatively brown before or after microwaving under a pre-heated conventional grill or oven.

Salt poultry after cooking to prevent drying out and toughening of the meat fibres.

Always *defrost* chicken *completely* before cooking and allow a suitable *defrosting*-standing time. The chart on page 39 gives appropriate times. The bird should be immersed in water during the *defrosting*-standing time for best results (see page 34).

To avoid overcooking of thin areas such as wing tips, cover these areas with small pieces of foil – follow guidance in your instruction book carefully on this.

Use wooden skewers or string to tie or truss a whole bird. Closing the body by trussing ensures even cooking.

Microwave whole birds, breast-side down for the first half of the cooking time. Turn the bird breast side up for the remainder. Allow whole birds and poultry dishes to rest for a *cooking*-standing time before serving. A whole bird requires 10–20 minutes covered with foil, after removal from the microwave oven.

Stuffed poultry will require a longer cooking time. Allow 1 minute extra per 450g/1 lb.

The following table may be used as a guide to cooking poultry. Allow a 15–20 minute *cooking*-standing time.

	Minutes per 450g/1 lb on HIGH
Chicken – whole	6–9
– portions	6–7
Duck – whole	7–8
Turkey – whole	7–9

A meat thermometer is a useful additional aid and instructions for its use are given on page 84.

TURKEY ROAST WITH REDCURRANT SAUCE

A different, rather special dish.

Serves: 4   *Freezer life: 2–3 months*

Cook: Turkey 12 minutes, sauce 4 minutes. *Cooking*-standing time: 10 minutes.
Defrost: 10 minutes. *Defrosting*-standing time: 5–10 minutes.
Reheat: 3–5 minutes.

	Met.	Imp.	Am.
Pre-packed turkey breast roast	600g	1¼ lb	1¼ lb
Redcurrant jelly	4 × 15ml sp	4 tbsp	4 tbsp
Onion, finely chopped	1 small	1 small	1 small
Button mushrooms, finely sliced	100g	4 oz	¼ lb
Salt and pepper			
Red wine	150ml	¼ pt	⅔ cup
Thyme, fresh sprig	1	1	1
or **dried**	2.5ml sp	½ tsp	½ tsp

Method
Defrost turkey if necessary, for about 8 minutes on DEFROST. Allow 5–10 minutes *defrosting*-standing time.

Place turkey roast in a suitable container, spread redcurrant jelly over the top, cover and cook for about 6 minutes on HIGH. Turn the turkey over, baste, cover and cook for a further 5–6 minutes. Remove the joint from its juices and allow to rest for a *cooking*-standing time of 10 minutes. Meanwhile stir the onion into the turkey juices, cover and cook on HIGH for 2 minutes. Stir in the mushrooms, seasoning, red wine and thyme. Cover and cook for 2 more minutes on HIGH.

Carve turkey into eight slices, arrange on serving dish and pour sauce over. Reheat in microwave if necessary for 2–3 minutes.

To serve: Good with sauté potatoes and green salad.
To freeze: Cool completely and freeze in the same container.
Defrost in same covered container on DEFROST for 10 minutes then allow a *defrosting*-standing time of 5 minutes. Reheat on HIGH for 3–5 minutes.

BARBECUE CHICKEN

The light texture of the chicken combines well with this tangy sauce, which also disguises the chicken's pale colour.

Serves: 4   *Freezer life: 1 month*

Cook: Chicken 12 minutes + 12 minutes, sauce 3 minutes + 8–10 minutes. *Cooking*-standing time: Chicken 15–20 minutes.
Defrost: Chicken 8–10 minutes, sauce 8–10 minutes. *Defrosting*-standing time: Chicken 10 minutes, sauce 10 minutes.
Reheat: Chicken 6–8 minutes, sauce 3–5 minutes.

	Met.	*Imp.*	*Am.*
Chicken, whole	1.4kg	3 lb	3 lb
Cooking oil	15ml sp	1 tbsp	1 tbsp
Onion, chopped finely			
or grated	1 small	1 small	1 small
Tomato ketchup	3–4×15ml sp	3–4 tbsp	3–4 tbsp
Mango chutney, chop			
if necessary	2×15ml sp	2 tbsp	2 tbsp
Mustard powder	5ml sp	1 tsp	1 tsp
Lemon juice or vinegar	2×15ml sp	2 tbsp	2 tbsp
Fine brown sugar	5ml sp	1 tsp	1 tsp
Worcestershire sauce	1–2×15ml sp	1–2 tbsp	1–2 tbsp
Salt and black pepper			

Method
DEFROST the chicken if necessary for about 20 minutes, allowing a *defrosting*-standing time of 30 minutes.

Brush the chicken with the cooking oil and place it, breast side down, in a large shallow dish. Cover and cook on HIGH for 12 minutes. Turn the bird breast side up, cover and cook for a further 12 minutes. Remove chicken, season it and wrap it in foil. Allow a *cooking*-standing time in the foil of 15–20 minutes. Strain the fat off the cooking juices and discard it. Add the onion to the cooking juices, cover and cook on HIGH for 3 minutes. Stir in the remaining ingredients and season with salt and black pepper. Cover and cook on HIGH for 8–10 minutes, stirring at least once during cooking. Unwrap the chicken and place on a hot serving dish. Pour the sauce over the chicken so that it is completely coated. Reheat for a few minutes if necessary.

Serve: With jacket or sauté potatoes or rice.

To freeze: Freeze chicken and sauce separately. Cool completely and freeze.

Defrost: Chicken on DEFROST for 8–10 minutes followed by a 10 minute *defrosting*-standing time; the sauce also needs to be on DEFROST for 8–10 minutes with its own 10 minute *defrosting*-standing time.

Reheat chicken on HIGH for 6–8 minutes; sauce on HIGH 3–5 minutes. Pour the sauce over the chicken as above.

PLUM DUCK

This is duck in a delicious, rich-coloured sauce; served with rice it is very suitable for a dinner.

Serves: 4   *Freezer life: 1–2 months*

Cook: Duck 12 minutes + 12 minutes + 5 minutes, sauce 8 minutes.
Cooking-standing time: Duck 10 minutes, sauce nil.
Defrost: Duck 15–20 minutes, sauce 6–8 minutes. *Defrosting*-standing time: Duck 10 minutes, sauce 5–10 minutes.
Reheat: Duck 10–15 minutes, sauce 3–5 minutes, plus extra if necessary.

	Met.	*Imp.*	*Am.*
Duck portions	4 × 400g	4 × 14 oz	4 × ¾ lb
Paprika	5ml sp	1 tsp	1 tsp
Hot water			
Sauce:			
Cornflour or cornstarch	2 × 15ml sp	2 tbsp	2 tbsp
Mustard powder	1 × 15ml sp	1 tbsp	1 tbsp
Grated rind of orange (optional)	1	1	1
Paprika	2 × 5ml sp	2 tsp	2 tsp
Orange juice, unsweetened	300ml	½ pt	1¼ cups
Plum jam	250g	8 oz	½ lb
Salt and black pepper			

Method
DEFROST the duck portions if necessary (approximately 20 minutes) and allow a 10 minute *defrosting*-standing time.

Sprinkle the 5ml/1 tsp paprika over the duck portions and arrange them on a roasting rack (or upturned plate) in a deep container. Cover with greaseproof paper and cook on HIGH for 12 minutes. Turn the duck pieces over, cover and cook on HIGH for a further 12 minutes. Again turn the duck pieces over, cover and cook on HIGH for about 5 minutes or until they are just cooked. Transfer the duck to a hot serving dish, cover securely with foil and leave for a *cooking*-standing time of 10 minutes.

Drain and discard the fat from the duck juices. Make the juices up to 300ml/½ pt/1¼ cups with hot water.

Sauce: Mix together in a suitable container or jug the cornflour, mustard powder, orange rind (optional) and paprika. Then stir in the orange juice, the duck juices/water and the plum jam. Season well with salt and black pepper. Cook on HIGH for 8 minutes, stirring at least twice during cooking, or until the sauce thickens.

Serve the duck portions with the sauce poured over them.

To freeze: Cool completely and freeze duck and sauce separately.

Defrost duck for 15-20 minutes on DEFROST followed by a 10 minute *defrosting*-standing time; sauce 6-8 minutes on DEFROST followed by a 5-10 minute *defrosting*-standing time.

Reheat duck portions on HIGH for 10-15 minutes, then the sauce for 3-5 minutes. Pour the sauce over the duck and reheat for a further few minutes if necessary.

QUICK-CURRIED TURKEY

A spicy way of using up left-over turkey or chicken. (*Remember:* Do not re-freeze cooked meat which has already been frozen.)

Serves: 4   *Freezer life: 1 month – only use fresh cooked meat if you intend to freeze this dish.*

Cook: 4 + 4 + 5 + 5 minutes. *Cooking*-standing time: 5-10 minutes.
Defrost: 10-15 minutes. *Defrosting*-standing time: 10 minutes.
Reheat: 8-10 minutes.

	Met.	Imp.	Am.
Turkey or chicken pieces,			
cooked	**400g**	**14 oz**	**¾ lb**
Butter or margarine	**15g**	**½ oz**	**1 tbsp**
Onion, chopped	**1 medium**	**1 medium**	**1 medium**

Curry powder	2 × 15ml sp	2 tbsp	2 tbsp
Flour	15ml sp	1 tbsp	1 tbsp
Chicken stock	550ml	1 pt	2½ cups
Tomato purée or paste	2 × 5ml sp	2 tsp	2 tsp
Lemon juice	15ml sp	1 tbsp	1 tbsp
Worcestershire sauce	2 × 15ml sp	2 tbsp	2 tbsp
Chutney	2 × 15ml sp	2 tbsp	2 tbsp
Sultanas	50g	2 oz	⅓ cup
Eating apple, peeled, cored and sliced	1	1	1
Salt and black pepper			

Method
DEFROST turkey pieces if necessary and allow for *defrosting*-standing time (see chart, page 39).

Place the butter and onion in a suitable container. Cover and cook on HIGH for 4 minutes. Stir in the curry powder and flour and gradually stir in the chicken stock; cover and cook on HIGH for 4 minutes or until it boils, stirring a few times during cooking. Add the remaining ingredients (except the turkey or chicken), cover and cook on HIGH for 5 minutes. Then stir in the turkey or chicken pieces, cover again and cook on HIGH for 5 minutes. Allow a *cooking*-standing time of 5–10 minutes.

To serve: With rice.
To freeze: Cool completely and freeze in same or microwave-freezer container.
To defrost: On DEFROST for 10–15 minutes. Allow a 10 minute *defrosting*-standing time.
Reheat on HIGH for 8–10 minutes.

RICE AND PASTA

Cooking times are similar to conventional times. The advantage of cooking rice and pasta by microwave is that its final texture is enhanced. Rice grains are separate and fluffy and pasta remains firm rather than becoming soft and soggy. The lack of steam in the kitchen and the fact that you can do away with sticky saucepans are extra plus points. An additional bonus is that rice and pasta can be reheated *very* successfully and simply in the microwave oven – a difficult job with conventional oven or hob.

Use a deep container which allows the rice or pasta to expand during cooking and allows the water to bubble up. Cover dishes with cling film during cooking, defrosting or reheating and remember to prick holes in the cover to allow steam to escape.

The chart on page 106 gives the approximate times for cooking *fresh* pasta and rice. Always allow for the *cooking*-standing time given. Left-over rice and pasta may be frozen and then defrosted and reheated at a later date. Defrosting times are followed by a *defrosting*-standing time. Follow the reheating times accurately to avoid over-cooking.

HADDOCK KEDGEREE

This attractive dish makes a substantial meal.

Serves: 4–6   *Freezer life: 1 month*

Cook: Fish 6½ minutes, rice 12 minutes, complete 4 minutes.
Cooking-standing time: Fish 5 minutes, rice 7 minutes.
Defrost: 5–8 minutes. *Defrosting*-standing time: 10 minutes.
Reheat: 6 minutes.

	Met.	*Imp.*	*Am.*
Smoked haddock	**450g**	**1 lb**	**1 lb**
Long grain rice	**350g**	**12 oz**	**¾ lb**
Chicken stock	**700ml**	**1¼ pt**	**3 cups**
Cooking oil	**¼ × 5ml sp**	**¼ tsp**	**¼ tsp**
Salt and pepper			
Hard-boiled eggs, chopped	**2**	**2**	**2**
Parsley, chopped	**15ml sp**	**1 tbsp**	**1 tbsp**
Butter	**50g**	**2 oz**	**4 tbsp**
Lemon wedges to garnish			

Method
DEFROST haddock if necessary. Do this in two stages. Microwave on DEFROST for 3–4 minutes followed by a 5 minute *defrosting*-standing time, then for a further 2–3 minutes on DEFROST followed by a further 5 minute *defrosting*-standing time.

Put the fish into a suitable shallow container. Cover and cook on HIGH for 6½ minutes, rearranging the pieces half way for even cooking results. Allow a *cooking*-standing time of 5 minutes.

In another suitable deep container cook the rice, stock, oil and seasoning on HIGH for 12 minutes. Allow a *cooking*-standing time of 7 minutes.

Flake the fish, discarding skin and bones. Stir the eggs, parsley, fish and butter (cut into pieces) into the rice. Adjust seasoning if necessary. Cover and cook for a further 4 minutes, stirring once.

Serve: Garnished with lemon wedges.
To freeze: Cool completely and freeze in a polythene bag.
Defrost for 5–8 minutes, breaking it up with a fork. Allow a *defrosting*-standing time of 10 minutes before reheating on HIGH for about 6 minutes.

RICE AND PASTA COOKING

	Cook on HIGH	Defrost	Reheat on HIGH
Savoury rice (dried) 100g/4 oz/¼ lb	Cook in 400ml/¾ pt/2 cups boiling salted water for 18 minutes. Cooking-standing time: 3 minutes.	4 minutes Defrosting-standing time: 2 minutes.	2 minutes Stand for 1 minute.
Long grain rice 225g/8 oz/½ lb	Cook in 550ml/1 pt/ 2½ cups boiling salted water for 9 minutes. Cooking-standing time: 5 minutes.	5 minutes Defrosting-standing time: 2 minutes.	4 minutes Stand for 2 minutes.
Brown rice 225g/8 oz/½ lb	Cook in 550ml/1 pt/2½ cups boiling salted water for 20 minutes. Cooking-standing time: 3–4 minutes.	7 minutes Defrosting-standing time: 2 minutes.	4–5 minutes Stand for 1 minute.
Egg noodles 225g/8 oz/½ lb	Cook in 550ml/1 pt/2½ cups boiling salted water for 5 minutes. Cooking-standing time: 2 minutes.	6 minutes Defrosting-standing time: 2 minutes.	5 minutes Stand for 1 minute.
Spaghetti 225g/8 oz/½ lb	Add 15ml sp/1 tbsp oil to 1.1 litre/ 2pts/5 cups boiling salted water and cook for 13 minutes. Cooking-standing time: 2 minutes.	6½ minutes Defrosting-standing time: 2 minutes.	4 minutes Stand for 2 minutes.

	Cook on HIGH	Defrost	Reheat on HIGH
Pasta shells 225g/8 oz/½ lb	Add 15ml sp/1 tbsp oil to 1.7 litre/ 3 pts/7½ cups boiling salted water and cook for 18 minutes. *Cooking*-standing time: 2 minutes.	7 minutes *Defrosting*-standing time: 2 minutes.	4 minutes Stand for 1 minute.
Macaroni 225g/8 oz/½ lb	Add 15ml sp/1 tbsp oil to 1.1 litre/ 2 pts/5 cups boiling salted water and cook for 8 minutes. *Cooking*-standing time: 2 minutes.	7 minutes *Defrosting*-standing time: 2 minutes.	4 minutes Stand for 1 minute.
Lasagne 225g/8 oz/½ lb	Cook in 1.1 litre/2 pts/5 cups boiling salted water for 4½ minutes. *Cooking*-standing time: 2 minutes	6 minutes *Defrosting*-standing time: 3 minutes.	4 minutes, turn around and over once Stand for 2 minutes.

BACON AND PRAWN RISOTTO

A memorable meal especially when eaten with crusty bread and a glass of red wine!

Serves: 4   *Freezer life: 1 month*

Cook: Vegetables 5 minutes, with rice and stock 10 minutes, complete 12–15 minutes. *Cooking*-standing time: 5 minutes. Defrost: 5–8 minutes. *Defrosting*-standing time: 10 minutes. Reheat: 6 minutes.

	Met.	Imp.	Am.
Butter	25g	1 oz	2 tbsp
Onion, finely chopped	1	1	1
Green pepper	1 small	1 small	1 small
Red pepper	1 small	1 small	1 small
Long grain rice	225g	8 oz	½ lb
Chicken stock, hot	750ml	1½ pts	3¾ cups
Back bacon, cut into strips	225g	8 oz	½ lb
Prawns, frozen	225g	8 oz	½ lb
Parsley, chopped	15ml sp	1 tbsp	1 tbsp

Method
Place the butter, onion and peppers in a suitable large deep container. Cover and cook on HIGH for 5 minutes. Add the rice and hot stock and then cook uncovered on HIGH for 10 minutes, stirring once. Add remaining ingredients, cover and cook on HIGH for a further 12–15 minutes. Allow a 5 minute *cooking*-standing time before serving.

Serve: See above.
To freeze: Cool completely and freeze in a polythene bag.
Defrost for 5–8 minutes, breaking it up with a fork. Allow a *defrosting*-standing time of 10 minutes before reheating on HIGH for about 6 minutes.

FRUIT AND DESSERTS

Desserts are delicious from the microwave oven. Sponge puddings and suet puddings are cooked in minutes instead of hours (when steaming conventionally). Puddings and custards are easy to cook in the microwave oven too. Cook milk puddings in an uncovered dish, allowing plenty of room for the milk to bubble up. Delicate puddings should be cooked on a low power setting, if you have one. Check with your instruction book. Packet mixes of custards, blancmanges and jellies are easily prepared in their serving dish.

Fruits cooked in the microwave oven are tender and juicy and retain maximum colour, flavour and nutrient content. Dried fruits such as apricots and prunes do not require overnight soaking before cooking. Prepare fruits for freezing too, (particularly cheap seasonal fruit), remembering to plan ahead and freeze in suitable quantities.

Points for microwaving fruit
Cook (or cut into) uniform pieces to encourage even cooking and arrange evenly in the container.

Cover fruit during microwave cooking.

Defrosting fruit is simple. Turn to the chart on page 40 for the appropriate times and *defrosting*-standing times.

Pierce the skins of whole fruit to prevent bursting.

To prepare fruit for freezing
Make a syrup (100g/4 oz/½ cup sugar and a pinch of ascorbic acid
to 300ml/½ pt/1¼ cups water) and heat on HIGH for about 5
minutes until the sugar has dissolved. Stir the syrup well and pour it
over the prepared fruit in a suitable microwave-freezer dish (make
sure it covers the fruit). Cover and microwave on HIGH for 1
minute. Then drain the fruit and cool completely before open
freezing, or cool completely in the syrup and freeze both together in
suitable serving quantities.

Cooking times for *fresh* fruit will vary with type. Check with your
instruction book. A general guide for cooking fresh fruit is:

Soft fruits: 2½–5 minutes on HIGH.
Hard fruits: 7–10 minutes on HIGH.

CRUNCHY ORANGE TRIANGLES

Here is a shortbread mixture with an unusual texture – a treat if
served with whipped cream flavoured with a little cointreau. An
alternative is to serve with Golden Pears (page 112).

Makes: 8   *Freezer life: 3 months*

Cook: 5 mins. *Cooking*-standing time: Completely cool.
Defrost: 2 minutes. *Defrosting*-standing time: 5 minutes.
Reheat: No need.

	Met.	Imp.	Am.
Butter	100g	4 oz	½ cup
Caster sugar	50g	2 oz	4 tbsp
Grated rind of orange	1	1	1
Plain flour, sifted	100g	4 oz	1 cup
Semolina	50g	2 oz	½ cup
Caster sugar to 'dust' top			

Method
Cream butter, sugar and orange rind until light and fluffy. Stir in
the sifted flour and semolina and work together with a wooden
spoon until blended. Butter a plate or suitable shallow dish and line
with greaseproof paper. Spread the mixture over to make a round
20cm/8 in diameter. Cook on HIGH for 5 minutes. Carefully mark

into triangles with a sharp knife. Sprinkle with sugar and leave to cool completely.

To serve: On its own, with whipped cream, or see above.
To freeze: Cool and interleave with polythene. Pack in a freezer bag, seal and freeze.
Defrost unpacked for 2 minutes on DEFROST and allow 5 minutes *defrosting*-standing time.

CINNAMON RHUBARB

This is delicious chilled with vanilla ice cream. Try serving with Crunchy Orange Triangles (above).

Serves: 4   *Freezer life: 9 months*

Cook: 9 minutes. *Cooking*-standing time: 5-10 minutes.
Defrost: 12 minutes. *Defrosting*-standing time: 10 minutes.
Reheat: Best chilled.

	Met.	*Imp.*	*Am.*
Rhubarb, cut into 2½cm/ 1 in lengths	700g	1½ lb	1 ½ lb
Soft brown sugar	50g	2 oz	4 tbsp
Cinnamon, ground	2.5ml sp	½ tsp	½ tsp
Cornflour or cornstarch	15ml sp	1 tbsp	1 tbsp
Rind and juice of lemon	1	1	1
Water	150ml	¼ pt	⅔ cup

Method
Arrange rhubarb in a suitable container. Mix together the sugar and cinnamon and sprinkle over the rhubarb. Mix together the remaining ingredients and pour over. Cover and cook on HIGH for 9 minutes (stir gently after 5 minutes). Leave for 5-10 minutes *cooking*-standing time.

To serve: Chill well – see above.
To freeze: Cool completely and freeze in same container.
Defrost: 12 minutes on DEFROST breaking up gently with a fork as it thaws, plus 10 minutes *defrosting*-standing time.

GOLDEN PEARS

The orange juice lifts the syrup sauce. Choose ripe but not soft pears – the cooking time will depend upon ripeness.

Serves: 4   *Freezer life: 1 month*

Cook: ½ minute softening, pears 3 minutes + 2 minutes.
Cooking-standing time: 5 minutes.
Defrost: 8 minutes. *Defrosting*-standing time: 5 minutes.
Reheat: About 3 minutes.

	Met.	*Imp.*	*Am.*
Pears	4	4	4
Golden syrup	4 × 15ml sp	4 tbsp	4 tbsp
Juice of orange	1 large	1 large	1 large
Orange, sliced	1	1	1

Method
Peel the pears, leaving them on their stalks. Put golden syrup in a suitable container and heat on HIGH for ½ minute to soften. Arrange the pears, stalks uppermost, in the container. Holding by the stalk, brush each pear with the syrup. Cover and cook on HIGH for 3 minutes. Sprinkle the orange juice over the pears and brush them again with syrup. Cover and cook on HIGH for 2 minutes, and allow a *cooking*-standing time of 5 minutes.

To serve: Hot or chilled with whipped cream and decorated with orange slices.
To freeze: Omit orange slices, cool completely and freeze in same container.
Defrost: 8 minutes, covered, on DEFROST plus 5 minutes *defrosting*-standing time. To serve the pears hot, reheat on HIGH for about 3 minutes.

PEARS IN CHOCOLATE SAUCE

The orange juice gives a 'tangy' taste to the chocolate sauce.

Serves: 4   *Freezer life: 1 month*

Cook: Pears 3 minutes + 2 minutes, sauce 1½ minutes. *Cooking-*

standing time: cool completely.
Defrost: Pears 5 minutes, sauce 2 minutes. *Defrosting*-standing
time: Pears 10 minutes, sauce 2 minutes.
Reheat: Sauce only, 1 minute.

	Met.	Imp.	Am.
Pears	4	4	4
Juice of oranges	2 medium	2 medium	2 medium
Plain (dark) chocolate	100g	4 oz	¼ lb
Chopped nuts (optional)			

Method
Peel the pears, leaving on the stalks. Put orange juice in a suitable
container and arrange the pears, stalks uppermost, in the container.
Holding the stalk, brush each pear with the orange juice. Cover and
cook on HIGH for 3 minutes. Brush the pears again, cover and
cook on HIGH for 2 minutes. Lift pears out of juice, arrange on a
serving dish, allow to cool completely and then chill. Break the
chocolate into the orange juice. Heat, uncovered, on HIGH for 1½
minutes and stir well until smooth and glossy.

To serve: Pour hot sauce over chilled pears.
To freeze: Cool and freeze pears and sauce separately.
Defrost pears for 5 minutes on DEFROST and allow 10 minutes
defrosting-standing time. DEFROST sauce for 2 minutes followed
by a 2 minute *defrosting*-standing time. Reheat sauce on HIGH
for 1 minute.

APRICOT SPONGE PUDDING

This is a simple fruity pudding. Jam or syrup may be used in place
of the fruit.

Serves: 4   *Freezer life: 3 months*

Cook: 3–5 minutes. *Cooking*-standing time: 5 minutes.
Defrost: 1½–2 minutes. *Defrosting*-standing time: 10 minutes.
Reheat: 1½–2 minutes.

	Met.	Imp.	Am.
Soft margarine	50g	2 oz	4 tbsp
Caster sugar	50g	2 oz	4 tbsp

Apricot Sponge Pudding—contd.

Egg (size 3) beaten	1	1	1
Self-raising flour	100g	4 oz	1 cup
Milk	45–60ml	3–4 tbsp	3–4 tbsp
Can apricot halves	411g	14½ oz	medium

Method
Beat together the margarine, sugar, egg and flour, adding sufficient milk to form a soft consistency which drops off the spoon.

Drain the apricots and arrange them in the base of a buttered 550ml/1 pt pudding dish. Spread the mixture over the top and level the surface. Cook uncovered on HIGH for 3–5 minutes or until the top is only slightly moist. Allow a 5 minute *cooking*-standing time.

Serve with custard or sweet white sauce or cream.
To freeze: Cool completely and wrap.
Defrost 1½–2 minutes on DEFROST followed by a 10 minute *defrosting*-standing time. Reheat on HIGH for 1½–2 minutes.

FREEZER/MICROWAVE SNACKS

Snacks are simply and quickly prepared in the microwave oven, at any time of the day. There is no need to heat up several appliances and use several plates and pans. Prepare your favourite snack in its serving dish. Small quantities of food can be taken from the freezer, fridge or store-cupboard to make hot tasty appetisers and snacks in minutes. Make them for freezing too so that you simply retrieve your portion from the freezer, defrost and then reheat in the microwave oven (e.g. savoury or sweet pancakes).

If your microwave oven has a browning grill or a browning dish, toasted and fried sandwiches are a favourite.

Reheat filled vols-aux-vents and bread rolls. Defrost and/or reheat individual portions of savoury flans or cooked pizza. Heat baked beans or cheese mixtures on slices of hot toast (particularly speedy if you have a toaster).

Here are a few of my favourite freezer/microwave snacks.

CHEESEBURGERS

A partiality of the youngsters in my home, these are easy to make.

Serves: 4   *Freezer life: Not suitable for freezing*

Cook: Beefburgers 6 minutes + 2–3 minutes. *Cooking*-standing time: 5 minutes.
Defrost:
Defrosting-standing time: } Will not keep frozen.
Reheat: Nil.

	Met.	Imp.	Am.
Beefburgers	4 × 100g	4 × 4 oz	4 × ¼ lb
Baps, split and buttered	4	4	4
Processed cheese slices	4	4	4
Salt and pepper			
Mustard relish	4 × 5ml sp	4 tsp	4 tsp

Method
DEFROST the beefburgers if necessary for about 6 minutes, allowing a 10 minute *defrosting*-standing time.

Place the beefburgers in a circle on a piece of paper towel on a plate. Cook on HIGH for 6 minutes. Allow a *cooking*-standing time of 5 minutes. Place the beefburgers in the buttered baps and top the meat in each one with a cheese slice. Season and spread on 5ml/tsp of mustard relish. Arrange the baps on the paper towel and cook on HIGH for 2–3 minutes, taking care not to over-heat (and therefore toughen) the bread.

GREEK MUSHROOMS

Delicious on hot toast or fried bread.

Serves: 4–6   *Freezer life: Not suitable*

Cook: Mushrooms and butter 5 minutes, with sauce and seasoning stirred in 4 minutes. *Cooking*-standing time: 5 minutes.
Defrost:
Defrosting-standing time: } Will not keep frozen.
Reheat: Nil.

	Met.	Imp.	Am.
Frozen mushrooms	450g	1 lb	1 lb
Butter	25g	1 oz	2 tbsp
Tomato purée or paste	3×15ml sp	3 tbsp	3 tbsp
Worcestershire sauce	2×5ml sp	2 tsp	2 tsp
Salt and black pepper			
Parsley, chopped	15ml sp	1 tbsp	1 tbsp

Method
Place the frozen mushrooms and butter in a suitable container, cover and cook on HIGH for 5 minutes, then stir in the tomato purée, Worcestershire sauce and plenty of seasoning. Cover and cook for a further 4 minutes, then allow a *cooking*-standing time of 5 minutes before stirring in the parsley.

CAULIFLOWER WITH CHEESE TOPPING

A light but filling snack which is easy to make.

Serves: 4   *Freezer life: Not suitable*

Cook: Cauliflower 12 minutes, with cheese 1 minute. *Cooking*-standing time: 7 minutes.
Defrost:
Defrosting-standing time: } Will not keep frozen.
Reheat: Nil.

	Met.	Imp.	Am.
Frozen cauliflower florets	450g	1 lb	1 lb
Water	30ml	2 tbsp	2 tbsp
Cheese, grated	100g	4 oz	¼ lb
Mustard powder	½ × 5ml sp	½ tsp	½ tsp
Salt and black pepper			

Method
Place the frozen cauliflower in a suitable container with the water.
Cover and cook on HIGH for 12 minutes, separating the florets two
or three times during the cooking. Then allow a *cooking*-standing
time of 7 minutes. Mix together the cheese and mustard powder.
Season the cauliflower and sprinkle the cheese mix over it. Cook on
HIGH for 1 minute.

JACKET POTATOES WITH YOGHURT AND CHIVE DRESSING

This makes a really warming snack on a winter's evening.

Serves: 4   *Freezer life: 3 months*

Cook: 10–15 minutes plus 1½ minutes. *Cooking*-standing time: 5
minutes.
Defrost: 5–8 minutes. *Defrosting*-standing time: 10 minutes.
Reheat: 3 minutes.

	Met.	Imp.	Am.
Potatoes	4 × 175g	4 × 6 oz	4 × 6 oz
Salt and black pepper			
Carton natural			
unsweetened yoghurt	150g	5 oz	small
Chives, chopped	2 × 15ml sp	2 tbsp	2 tbsp

Method
Prick the potatoes well with a fork. Arrange them on a paper towel
in the microwave oven. Cook on HIGH for 10–15 minutes, turning
the potatoes over once. Wrap the potatoes in foil and allow a
cooking-standing time of 5 minutes. Split the potatoes in half,
scoop out the potato from their centres and mash it. Mix the

remaining ingredients with the potato mash and pack the mixture back into the skins. Cook on HIGH for 1½ minutes.

To freeze: Omit the final 1½ minutes cooking. Cool the potato halves completely before freezing.
Defrost for 5–8 minutes and allow a 10 minute *defrosting*-standing time before reheating on HIGH for about 3 minutes.

COOKING FOR ONE AND TWO

This section concentrates on individuals or couples, young or old – who want speedy, economical, but nutritiously satisfying meals from the freezer and store cupboard. The following recipes form a collection which should inspire additional experimentation to please personal tastes.

When cooking to freeze, any of the other recipes in this book may also be prepared and frozen in individual portions to be defrosted and reheated in minutes. Simply follow the general defrost/reheat instructions at the end of each recipe and adjust the time to suit your oven.

Cooking times for the following recipes should be adjusted when cooking extra portions. Add 50% more time per portion when cooking for up to four people. For example if one portion takes 2 minutes four portions should take 5 minutes.

Baby food
Small amounts of food for baby are economically cooked, defrosted and/or reheated in the microwave oven. They can be cooked in bulk quantities, divided into individual portions (e.g. ice cube trays) before freezing for use at a later date. This is a simple way of ensuring that your infant has a varied (and therefore balanced) diet. Remember – food gets very hot in a microwave oven, *so test it carefully before feeding to baby.*

SPICY BEEFBURGER

This provides a quick tasty lunch or snack and is ideal for the unexpected visitor too.

Serves: 1   *Freezer life: Not suitable for freezing.*

Defrost: 2 minutes. *Defrosting*-standing time: 2 minutes.
Cook: 1½–2 minutes. *Cooking*-standing time: 2 minutes.
Reheat: Nil.

	Met.	*Imp.*	*Am.*
Frozen beefburger or hamburger	100g	4 oz	¼ lb
Tomato ketchup or sauce	5ml sp	1 tsp	1 tsp
Chutney	2 × 5ml sp	2 tsp	2 tsp
French mustard	5ml sp	1 tsp	1 tsp
Brown sugar	pinch	pinch	pinch

Method
DEFROST beefburger or hamburger for 2 minutes, and then leave for 2 minutes *defrosting*-standing time. Mix together remaining ingredients and spread mixture over the beefburger or hamburger. Cook on HIGH for 1½–2 minutes. A *cooking*-standing time of 2 minutes thereafter is adequate before serving.

Serve with a green or mixed salad and crusty bread or a bread roll, or with pitta bread and cream cheese.

FISH IN BARBECUE SAUCE

This is fish with a 'bite'.

Serves: 1   *Freezer life: Not suitable for freezing*

Defrost: 2 minutes. *Defrosting*-standing time: 2 minutes.
Cook: 1 minute + 30 seconds. *Cooking*-standing time: 1 minute.
Reheat: Nil.

	Met.	Imp.	Am.
Pre-packed frozen cod or haddock portion	92g	3¼ oz	Small
Butter			
Salt and pepper			
Tomato ketchup or sauce	15ml sp	1 tbsp	1 tbsp
Vinegar	5ml sp	1 tsp	1 tsp
Mango chutney	15ml sp	1 tbsp	1 tbsp
Dry mustard	pinch	pinch	pinch
Sugar	2.5ml sp	½ tsp	½ tsp
Worcestershire sauce	2 × 5ml sp	2 tsp	2 tsp

Method

DEFROST fish portion for 2 minutes and allow 2 minutes *defrosting*-standing time. Then dot fish with butter, season lightly and place in a suitable container, cover and cook on HIGH for 1 minute. Remove. Mix remaining ingredients in a small basin. Spread over fish, cover and cook for another 30 seconds. Allow 1 minute *cooking*-standing time before serving.

To serve: With rice, pasta (see chart on page 106) or a simple green salad.

CHICKEN WITH HERB BUTTER

Use other flavourings, e.g. honey and lemon juice, tomato juice or commercially prepared barbecue seasoning, if you prefer.

Serves: 1   *Freezer life: 1 month*

Defrost: 4–5 minutes. *Defrosting*-standing time: 15 minutes.
Cook: 4 minutes. *Cooking*-standing time: 5 minutes.
Reheat: 2 minutes.

	Met.	Imp.	Am.
Frozen *uncooked* chicken			
portions, skinned	1 × 225g	1 × 8 oz	1 × ½ lb
Butter	15g	½ oz	1 tbsp
Black pepper			
Dried tarragon	¼ × 5ml sp	¼ tsp	¼ tsp
Salt			

Method
DEFROST chicken portions on HIGH for 4–5 minutes and allow a
15 minute *defrosting*-standing time. Dot the butter over the chicken
placed in a suitable small container. Sprinkle black pepper and
tarragon over it. Cover and cook on HIGH for about 4 minutes,
then allow a *cooking*-standing time of 5 minutes before seasoning
with salt. To reheat the chicken if necessary, microwave on HIGH
for about 2 minutes.

Serve with vegetables or salad.
The dish may be frozen after letting it cool off completely.
Defrost for 4–5 minutes plus 15 minutes *defrosting*-standing time.
Reheat for 2 minutes.

LAMB CHOP SPECIAL

A very tasty way of preparing lamb chops.

Serves: 1   *Freezer life: Not applicable*

Defrost: 2–3 minutes. *Defrosting*-standing time 10 minutes.
Cook: 3 minutes. *Cooking*-standing time: 5 minutes.
Reheat: 1–2 minutes.

	Met.	Imp.	Am.
Frozen loin lamb chop	1	1	1
Mint jelly	15ml sp	1 tbsp	1 tbsp
Mushrooms, chopped or			
sliced	25g	1 oz	1 oz
Salt and pepper			

Method
DEFROST lamb chop for 2–3 minutes, depending on size, and
allow a 10 minute *defrosting*-standing time. Place the chop in a

suitable small container. Spread the mint jelly over it and sprinkle the mushrooms on top. Cover and cook on HIGH for about 3 minutes and allow a 5 minute *cooking*-standing time. Season with salt and pepper. Reheat on HIGH for 1–2 minutes if needed.

Serve: With green salad and jacket potato.

DEVILLED KIDNEYS

It takes only 10 minutes to prepare this traditional dish in the microwave.

Serves: 2   *Freezer life: 2 months*

Cook: Onion 2 minutes, kidneys 4 + 1 minutes. *Cooking*-standing time: 5 minutes.
Defrost: 4–5 minutes. *Defrosting*-standing time: 10 minutes.
Reheat: 3–4 minutes.

	Met.	Imp.	Am.
Butter	25g	1 oz	2 tbsp
Spring onions, chopped	4	4	4
Lamb's kidneys, sliced	6	6	6
Salt and pepper			
Worcestershire sauce	15ml sp	1 tbsp	1 tbsp
Sherry	15ml sp	1 tbsp	1 tbsp
Parsley, chopped	2 × 5ml sp	2 tsp	2 tsp

Method
Place the butter and spring onions in a suitable container, cover and cook on HIGH for 2 minutes. Stir in the kidneys, cover and cook on HIGH for 4 minutes, stirring once. Add the remaining ingredients and cook on HIGH for 1 minute. Allow a *cooking*-standing time of 5 minutes.

To serve: On toast or rice or with croûtons.
To freeze: Cool completely and freeze in a microwave-freezer container.
Defrost for 4–5 minutes on DEFROST and allow a *defrosting*-standing time of 10 minutes.
Reheat covered on HIGH for 3–4 minutes.

INDEX

A

About the recipes, 46, 47
Adapting own recipes, 15 *et seq.*
Advantages of microwave oven, 10, 11
Apple, bacon and, pudding, 88
Apricot sponge pudding, 113

B

Baby food, 44, 119
Bacon and apple pudding, 88
        prawn risotto, 108
Barbecue chicken, 100
Basic white sauce, 77
Beefburger, spicy, 119
Blanching chart, vegetables, 66 *et seq.*
   vegetables, 65
Boeuf bourgignon, 90
Braised Chinese leaves, 73
Brandied lamb's liver pâté, 56
Browning dish/skillet, 30, 72
   grill/element, 20, 25

C

Casseroled bacon and butter beans, 86
Cauliflower with cheese topping, 116
Chantilly peas, 76
Cheeseburgers, 115
Chicken with herb butter, 120
Chinese chicken soup, 55
Chips, oven, 72

Choosing a microwave oven, 18 *et seq.*
Cinnamon rhubarb, 111
Cleaning, 11, 21
Combination microwave cookers, 19
Conduction, 13
Containers, 16, 21, 25 *et seq.*
   – suitability for use, 25
Controls, 11
Convection, 13
Convenience of microwave oven, 11
Conventional cooking, 13
Conversion tables, 48, 49
Cooking for one and two, 118 *et seq.*
   times, 15, 46
Cooking-standing time, 15
Creamy kipper appetiser, 57
   thick tomato soup, 52
Crunchy orange triangles, 110

D

Defrost control, 20
Defrosting bread, 42
   cakes, 41
   checkpoints, 33 *et seq.*
   desserts, 40
   fish, 36
   fruit, 40
   guide, 32 *et seq.*
   meat, 37
   pastry, 41
   poultry, 39
   rice, 40
   vegetables, 40

Defrosting-standing time, 32
Desserts, fruit and, 109 *et seq.*
Devilled kidneys, 122
Double-oven microwave cookers, 19
Duck, plum, 101

E

Economy, 10
Equipment to use, 25 *et seq.*
Escalopes of veal with orange, 94

F

Fast-freeze switch, 23
Fish, 58 *et seq.*
 , cooking fresh, 59
 in barbecue sauce, 120
 curry sauce, 62
 , poached, with cucumber, 61
 , smoked, in shells, 59
Foil, 21, 27, 84, 98
Freezer, 23 *et seq.*
 checkpoints, 25
 /microwave snacks, 114 *et seq.*
 vegetable soup, 54
Freezing food, 23
Fruit and desserts, 109 *et seq.*
Fruity sauce, 81

G

Gingery mince with dumplings, 84
Golden pears, 112
Goulash, lamb, 92

Greek mushrooms, 116

H

Haddock kedgeree, 105
 veronique, 60
Heart pacemakers, 12

J

Jacket potatoes with yoghurt and chive dressing, 117

L

Lamb chop special, 121
 chops in fruity sauce, 95
 goulash, 92
Leek parcels in cheesy sauce, 74
Limitations of microwave oven, 11, 12
Liver and bacon, savoury, 89

M

Mackerel in cider, 63
Magnetron, 18, 21
Meat, 82 *et seq.*
 cooking times, 84
 thermometers, 84
Meatballs, savoury, in tomatoes, 91
Memory controls, 20
Metal containers, 14, 21
Microwave/freezer friendship, 9
 snacks, 114 *et seq.*
 oven, 13 *et seq.*

, advantages of, 10, 11
, care of, 21 *et seq.*
, choosing a, 18 *et seq.*
, cleaning, 11, 21
, convenience of, 11
, limitations of, 11, 12
, thermometers, 30, 31,
   34
Microwaves, 13, 14
Mince, gingery, with dumplings, 84
Minerals, 11
Mixed meats loaf, 93
Mushroom and onion soup, 53
Mushrooms, Greek, 116

N

Nutty butterscotch sauce, 80

O

Orange chocolate sauce, 81
Oven chips, 72

P

Pacemakers, 12
Parsnip and leek soup, 51
Pasta, rice and, 104
Pears, golden, 112
   in chocolate sauce, 112
Plum duck, 101
Poached fish with cucumber, 61
Pork and mushroom cream, 87
   fricassée, 96
Poultry, 97 *et seq.*

Q

Quick-curried turkey, 102

R

Radiation, 13
Reheating, 43 *et seq.*
   fish, 58
   times, 43
Rhubarb, cinnamon, 111
Rice and pasta, 104
Roasting racks, 30, 83, 98

S

Sauces, 77 *et seq.*
Savoury liver and bacon, 89
   meatballs in tomatoes, 91
   onion and parsnip bake, 72
Seasoning, 16
Soups and starters, 50 *et seq.*
   , canned, 50
   , dried, 51
Speed of microwave cookery,
   10
Spicy beefburger, 119
   tomato sauce, 78
Star ratings, 23
Starters, soups and, 50 *et seq.*
Sweet'n'sour sauce, 79

T

Tabletop microwave ovens, 18
Temperature probe/sensor, 20,
   31
Thermometers, 30, 31, 34
   , meat, 84
Tomato sauce, spicy, 78
Turkey, quick-curried, 102
   roast with redcurrant sauce,
   99
Turntable, 19, 34, 44, 47
Two-level microwave ovens, 18

V

Variable power, 20
Veal, escalopes of, with orange,
    94
Vegetable blanching chart, 66
    et seq.
    soup, freezer, 54
Vegetables, 64 et seq.
    , blanching, 65

, canned, 65
, fresh, 65
, frozen, 68 et seq.
Versatility, 10
Vitamins, 11, 65

W

White sauce, basic, 77

OTHER GREAT PAPERFRONT BOOKS

Each uniform with this book

MICROWAVE COOKING PROPERLY EXPLAINED

Annette Yates' first book shows how the versatile microwave oven, on its own, can transform life for the busy cook.
Includes over 90 recipes which complement those in this
book, each personally tested by the author and her family.

DEEP FREEZE SECRETS

Explains all aspects of freezer ownership – from initial
purchase to bulk buying in order to cut costs. Includes ideas
for "instant" meals, taken out of the freezer and ready to eat
without any preparation, along with many other recipes.

BASIC FREEZER RECIPES

Includes almost 150 mouth-watering recipes. Details
storage times and space taken up by each item. Save time,
money and work by using your freezer in the most effective
way.

FOOD PROCESSORS PROPERLY EXPLAINED

Dianne Page shows how this kitchen wizard can improve your cooking expertise. Includes a large recipe section – all of which she has tested herself.

EASYMADE WINE AND COUNTRY DRINKS

As little as a few pence a bottle can be the cost of wines made from these straightforward country recipes which have stood the test of time. The ingredients can be easily found in field and hedgerow. No expensive equipment is required.

Includes a wine calendar to let you know when to make each wine throughout the year.

WINE MAKING THE NATURAL WAY

As its title suggests, this book concentrates on making wine from natural ingredients, without using chemical additives. Each recipe also includes details of how to make sugar-free wine.

HANDBOOK OF HERBS

Chapters deal with different herbs, giving recipes for their use, medicinal properties, how to grow them and so on. Also included is a chapter mentioning various spices, which gives similar information.

ELLIOT RIGHT WAY BOOKS
KINGSWOOD, SURREY, U.K.

OUR PUBLISHING POLICY

HOW WE CHOOSE

Our policy is to consider every deserving manuscript and we can give special editorial help where an author is an authority on his subject but an inexperienced writer. We are rigorously selective in the choice of books we publish. We set the highest standards of editorial quality and accuracy. This means that a *Paperfront* is easy to understand and delightful to read. Where illustrations are necessary to convey points of detail, these are drawn up by a subject specialist artist from our panel.

HOW WE KEEP PRICES LOW

We aim for the big seller. This enables us to order enormous print runs and achieve the lowest price for you. Unfortunately, this means that you will not find in the *Paperfront* list any titles on obscure subjects of minority interest only. These could not be printed in large enough quantities to be sold for the low price at which we offer this series. We sell almost all our *Paperfronts* at the same unit price. This saves a lot of fiddling about in our clerical departments and helps us to give you world-beating value. Under this system, the longer titles are offered at a price which we believe to be unmatched by any publisher in the world.

OUR DISTRIBUTION SYSTEM

Because of the competitive price, and the rapid turnover, *Paperfronts* are possibly the most profitable line a bookseller can handle. They are stocked by the best bookshops all over the world. It may be that your bookseller has run out of stock of a particular title. If so, he can order more from us at any time—we have a fine reputation for "same day" despatch, and we supply any order, however small (even a single copy), to any bookseller who has an account with us. We prefer you to buy from your bookseller, as this reminds him of the strong underlying public demand for *Paperfronts*. Members of the public who live in remote places, or who are housebound, or whose local bookseller is unco-operative, can order direct from us by post.

FREE

If you would like an up-to-date list of all paperfront titles currently available, send a stamped self-addressed envelope to
ELLIOT RIGHT WAY BOOKS, BRIGHTON RD.,
LOWER KINGSWOOD, SURREY, U.K.